CHOSEN FOR CHILDREN

1936 – 1957

Arthur Ransome
The first author to receive the Library Association Carnegie Medal

Chosen for Children

An account of the books which have been awarded the *Library Association Carnegie Medal*, 1936–1957

THE LIBRARY ASSOCIATION

1957

Published by The Library Association,
Chaucer House, Malet Place, London,
in 1957,
to mark the twenty-first anniversary
of the institution of
The Library Association Carnegie Medal

DESIGNED AND PRINTED BY W. S. COWELL LTD, BUTTER MARKET, IPSWICH

CONTENTS

		PAGE
The Library Association Carnegie Medal		I
1936.	*Pigeon Post*, by Arthur Ransome	3
1937.	*The Family from One End Street*, by Eve Garnett	9
1938.	*The Circus is Coming*, by Noel Streatfeild	14
1939.	*Radium Woman*, by Eleanor Doorly	17
1940.	*Visitors from London*, by Kitty Barne	21
1941.	*We Couldn't Leave Dinah*, by Mary Treadgold	25
1942.	*The Little Grey Men*, by BB	30
1943.	No award	
1944.	*The Wind on the Moon*, by Eric Linklater	35
1945.	No award	
1946.	*The Little White Horse*, by Elizabeth Goudge	40
1947.	*Collected Stories for Children*, by Walter de la Mare	45
1948.	*Sea Change*, by Richard Armstrong	50
1949.	*The Story of Your Home*, by Agnes Allen	54
1950.	*The Lark on the Wing*, by Elfrida Vipont	57
1951.	*The Wool-pack*, by Cynthia Harnett	62
1952.	*The Borrowers*, by Mary Norton	66
1953.	*A Valley Grows Up*, by Edward Osmond	70
1954.	*Knight Crusader*, by Ronald Welch	74
1955.	*The Little Bookroom*, by Eleanor Farjeon	78
1956.	*The Last Battle*, by C. S. Lewis	83
Another Medal		88

ACKNOWLEDGEMENTS

Thanks are due to the writers who have contributed to this book, to Marcus Crouch for compiling it, and also to the following publishers for permission to reproduce some of the text and illustrations of Carnegie Medal Books and for the loan of blocks:

THE BODLEY HEAD LTD: An extract from *The Last Battle* and illustrations by Pauline Baynes on pages vii and 84.

JONATHAN CAPE LTD: Extracts from *Pigeon Post* and *We Couldn't Leave Dinah* and the illustration by Stuart Tresilian on page 27.

J. M. DENT AND SONS LTD: Extracts from *The Circus is Coming, Visitors from London, Sea Change* and *The Borrowers*, and two illustrations by Ruth Gervis on pages 22 and 24, an illustration by M. Leszczynski on page 52, and an illustration by Diana Stanley on page 67.

EYRE AND SPOTTISWOODE LTD AND MR D. J. WATKINS-PITCHFORD: An extract, one illustration and an initial letter from *The Little Grey Men* on pages 32 and 33.

FABER AND FABER LTD: Extracts from *Collected Stories for Children* and *The Story of Your Home*, and an illustration by Agnes and Jack Allen from the latter book on page 56.

WILLIAM HEINEMANN LTD: An extract from *The Radium Woman* and two illustrations by Robert Gibbings on pages vii and 18.

MACMILLAN AND CO. LTD: An extract from *The Wind on the Moon* and an illustration by Nicolas Bentley on page 38.

METHUEN AND CO. LTD: An extract from *The Wool-pack* and the illustration by Cynthia Harnett on page 64.

FREDERICK MULLER LTD: An extract from *The Family from One End Street* and the illustration by Eve Garnett on page 9.

OXFORD UNIVERSITY PRESS: Extracts from *The Lark on the Wing*, *A Valley Grows Up*, *Knight Crusader* and *The Little Bookroom*, and the illustration by T. R. Freeman on page 58, the illustration by Edward Osmond on page 73, the illustration by William Stobbs on page 76 and two illustrations by Edward Ardizzone on the title page and page 78.

UNIVERSITY OF LONDON PRESS: An extract from *The Little White Horse* and two illustrations by C. Walter Hodges on pages 42 and 43.

THE EDITOR OF *The Junior Bookshelf* AND DR ARTHUR RANSOME: For the letter on page 5.

Acknowledgements are also due for the use of photographs as follows:
Arthur Ransome and Mary Treadgold (Jonathan Cape Ltd), Kitty Barne, Richard Armstrong and Mary Norton (J. M. Dent and Sons Ltd), B.B. (Eyre and Spottiswoode Ltd), Eric Linklater (Macmillan and Co. Ltd), Elizabeth Goudge (Tom Blau), Walter de la Mare (Faber and Faber Ltd, and Mark Gerson), Agnes Allen (Faber and Faber Ltd, and Elliott and Fry), Elfrida Vipont (Oxford University Press and Bryan Homer of Kendal), Cynthia Harnett (Methuen and Co. Ltd), Edward Osmond and Ronald Welch (Oxford University Press), and C. S. Lewis (Gillman and Soame).

THE LIBRARY ASSOCIATION
CARNEGIE MEDAL

THE Carnegie Medal was founded in 1936 in commemoration of the centenary of the birth of Andrew Carnegie, and the first award was made in the following year to Arthur Ransome.

The award is made annually for 'an outstanding book for children by a British subject domiciled in the United Kingdom (Great Britain and Northern Ireland) published during the preceding year.' The selection is made by a Sub-committee of the Library Association, who are guided in their choice by recommendations received from members of the Association.

In two of the war years the award was withheld for lack of a book of suitable quality. In the twenty-one years of the Medal's existence, therefore, it has been awarded nineteen times. Eleven of the recipients have been women. For the most part, the Medal has gone to writers who are known principally for their work for children, and generally to those who are established writers. Three of the winning books have been non-fictional, five have been fantasies, seven stories of contemporary life, two historical novels, and two collections of short stories. The Medal has not yet been awarded for a book of poetry.

The shelf of Carnegie Medal winners shows a varied collection of books. It may no doubt be assumed that the Sub-committee have not been concerned with variety. They have in fact been seeking distinction. It is the elusiveness of distinction, a quality which is not susceptible of definition, combined with the lack of limitations, which makes it so unlikely that every decision of the Sub-committee will receive universal approval. In the average year's output of some 1,500 children's books, several may well show distinctive qualities; in making a choice from these, the Sub-committee may favour a book by an author whose previous books have been admirable, or one which covers a subject for which there is an unsatisfied demand, or one which has an original approach. The recent practice of publishing a list of 'runners-up' has helped to make the Sub-committee's standards more clear; it has dispelled the idea that the Carnegie Medal winner stands alone in splendid isolation.

Critics have sometimes faulted the assessors for awarding the Medal to a writer whose appeal is to a rather limited audience. This is to apply the democratic principle blindly. The Medal is not awarded as the result of a plebiscite; it is awarded by a small body of experts who bring to the assessment of the eligible books high standards of criticism and long experience of books and their readers. These judges are unlikely to be attracted by facile or meretricious qualities. This is not to say that the Carnegie Medal books are unpopular with children. A book for children, however excellent in style, integrity and accuracy, is a failure if it lacks the elusive quality of personality which makes it acceptable to its audience. This is the quality shared by all the finest children's books; it is perhaps the one thing common to all the Medal-winners. It would however be as unlikely that such books, which make demands on the imagination and the concentration of their readers, should enjoy the widest popularity as that the novels of Virginia Woolf and E. M. Forster should be the most popular of adult books. A test of the good children's book, as of a book for adults, is that it receives the commendation of discriminating readers.

After twenty-one years the Carnegie Medal remains the only official tribute in this country to good writing and publishing for children. Its influence, though still small, is not to be despised. There have been marked improvements since 1936 in the general standard of publishing and reviewing of children's books. It is not too much to claim that this is attributable in part to an acceptance of the high standards established by the Carnegie Medal.

1936

ARTHUR RANSOME

Pigeon Post

illustrated by the author JONATHAN CAPE

ALTHOUGH 1936 was a good year for children's books, there could have been little doubt on whom the first choice for the Carnegie Medal should fall. The natural choice was the writer who, six years earlier, had ushered in a new era with *Swallows and Amazons*. *Pigeon Post*, if not Arthur Ransome's best book, was rich in the qualities which distinguished all his work. The Carnegie Medal got off to a good start with a book which had style, meaning and pace, and which was firmly based on sound social and aesthetic values.

In *Pigeon Post* the Swallows, the Amazons and the D's are again on holiday in Lakeland. They were never children to do things by halves, and in this story they have taken to mining and pigeon-training with their own blend of enthusiasm and common sense. They camp out, prospect for gold, outwit a competitor, and in a final episode mobilize the countryside to fight a forest fire. In the course of the story they develop their characteristic self-discipline, exercise a great deal of practical ingenuity, and carry out with varying degrees of success a number of technical experiments.

One of the great charms of Dr Ransome's children is their absorption in their various occupations. They are among the most unself-conscious of all fictional children. Each is a highly individual person, carefully observed; each grows and develops through contact with the others and with circumstance. Although they are all beautifully drawn full-length portraits, Dick's is perhaps the most finely conceived. Dick is the clever, bookish boy who in lesser hands would have become an impractical clown; Dr Ransome shows how valuable his kind of intelligence can be in solving practical problems.

For the first time since *Bevis*, the children's book became, with Dr Ransome, intensely concerned with everyday things. There are exciting

3

adventures in *Pigeon Post*, but they are adventures of everyday (or holiday) life. As Eric Linklater says of a later book (*Great Northern?*): 'He makes a tale of adventure a handbook to adventure', and wonderful practical hand-books they can be to self-reliant sensible children in getting the best out of a country holiday. The curious drawings have been often misjudged be-cause of their lack of artistic merit; they are in fact working drawings and are in the exact sense 'illustrations'.

from Chapter XV

She found the twig at once and picked it up by the point of the fork, putting off to the very last minute the holding of those two ends in her hands. But perhaps it would not work, anyway.

Titty swallowed once or twice. No one was here to see. No one would know if, after all, she could not bring herself to do it.

'Oh, come on,' she said to herself. 'You've got to. Better get it over.'

She turned the twig round and took the two ends, one in each hand just as Nancy had shown her by Mrs Tyson's pump. She found herself breathing very fast.

'Duffer,' she said firmly. 'You can just drop it if you want.'

She began walking to and fro across the level platform of the old fire spot. Nothing happened.

'Idiot,' she said. 'It won't be here, anyway.'

She left the platform and went in among the trees, looking in the dim light for Dick's green rushes. She found a tuft of them. Still nothing happened.

'It's all right,' she said to herself. 'You can't do it. It was only accident the other night. Nothing to be afraid of anyway. And you've tried. So it isn't your fault . . .'

And then she nearly dropped the twig. There it was, that tickling. Faint. Not like that other night at Tyson's. But the same thing. The twig was trying to move.

For a long time she stood where she was, somehow not daring to stir. Then she took a step or two, and the stick was as dead as ever.

'This is silly,' she said, and stepped back to the place where she had been and felt the stick press against the balls of her thumbs just as it had before.

'Well, it can't bite you,' said Titty, and made herself walk to and fro, in and out among the bushes and low trees at the edge of the wood just as she had on the open platform of Might Have Been.

The twig was moving again. Again it stopped. Again it twitched in her fingers.

'There *is* water here,' said Titty to herself. 'There must be. Unless it's all rot, like Dick thought.'

She walked slowly on. The twig was pulling harder and harder. She wanted to throw it down, but, somehow, by herself, she was not as frightened of it as she had been when, all unexpectedly, she had felt it for the first time. No one was watching her now, for one thing. She had won her battle the moment she had brought herself to hold the twig again. Now, already, she was almost eagerly feeling the pulling of the twig. When it weakened she moved back until she felt it strengthen. Then again she walked on. It was like looking for something hidden, while someone, who knew where it was, called out hot or cold as she moved nearer to or further from the hiding place.

Suddenly, as she came nearer the Great Wall, the twisting of the twig became more violent. Here was a shallow dip in the ground between two rocks, and, yes, there was another tuft of those rushes in the bottom of it. She walked in between the rocks and it was just as it had been in the farmyard at Tyson's. The stick seemed to leap in her hands. The ends of it pressed against her thumbs, while the point of the fork dipped towards the ground, bending the branches, twisting her hands round with them, and at last almost springing out of her fingers.

It's here,' said Titty. 'I've found it.'   *Pigeon Post*, pp 154–6

ARTHUR RANSOME was born in Leeds in 1884, the son of Professor Cyril Ransome. He was educated at Rugby, spending most of his holidays in the Lake District. As a journalist he travelled in Europe and Asia and was in Russia during the Revolution. His wife is Russian. He has written literary criticism, including an important book on Oscar Wilde (1912), and books on a great many subjects, of which *Racundra's First Cruise* (1923) is perhaps the most memorable. His many interests, particularly sailing and fishing, are reflected in the twelve 'Swallows and Amazons' books published between 1930 and 1947. He is a notable broadcaster. He holds an honorary Doctorate of Leeds University. In 1953 he received the C.B.E.

A LETTER TO THE EDITOR

(Reprinted from *The Junior Bookshelf*, Vol. 1, Number 4)

Yacht 'Nancy Blackett'
April, 1937

Dear Mr Woodfield,

You asked for an article, but, sitting here in my little cabin, with the coke glowing red in the stove, a kettle simmering, and old Nancy, in from the sea, lying quietly on her moorings, I don't feel like writing anything so formal. You wouldn't yourself, if you had been up at five in the morning and spent the whole long day beating to windward. You must forgive me for writing a letter instead. I will try to keep to the subjects you suggest.

First: on writing books for children. I do not know how to write books for children and have the gravest doubts as to whether anybody should try to do any such thing. To write a book *for* children seems to me a sure way of writing what is called a 'juvenile', a horrid, artificial thing, a patronizing thing, a thing that betrays in every line that author and intended victims are millions of miles apart, and that the author is enjoying not the stuff of his book but a looking-glass picture of himself or herself 'being so good with children' . . . a most unpleasant spectacle for anyone who happens to look over his shoulder. It is true that some of the best children's books were written with a particular audience in view – *Alice in Wonderland* and *The Wind in the Willows*, for example. Many others were not, and it is impossible to read even those that were without realizing that one member of that audience, and the one whose taste had dictatorial rights, was the author. Lewis Carroll was not 'writing down' further than to Lewis Carroll, and though Kenneth Grahame could count on a delighted listener in his small son, the first person to enjoy the exquisite fun of Mr Toad and his friends was Kenneth Grahame himself. Stevenson was stimulated to the writing of *Treasure Island* by the presence of a young stepson, greedy for the chapters as they came, but his first delighted public was Robert Louis Stevenson. 'If this don't fetch the kids,' he writes, 'why, they have gone rotten since my day.' And, 'It's awful fun, boys' stories; you just indulge the pleasure of your heart. . . .' That, it seems to me, is the secret. You just indulge the pleasure of your heart. You write not *for* children but for yourself, and if, by good fortune, children enjoy what you enjoy, why then you are a writer of children's books. . . . No special credit to you, but simply thumping good luck. Every writer wants to have readers, and than children there are no better readers in the world.

6

Second: the country of my own books. Stevenson talks somewhere of the importance of maps, and says you should know the country of your tales 'like your hand'. If you know a bit of country really well, it takes a very active part in the making of your book. You can count on it. It is always there and, somehow or other, life flows from it into your story. In the case of one of my books, the country is that of the Norfolk Broads, where I had an enormous lot of pleasure during the years when I was too groggy to go to sea. In the case of another, I worked out with a fair amount of accuracy the proper course for a small sailing vessel between Lowestoft and the Caribbees. The one I am now busy on is about the North Sea, and I let my own little ship blow across to Holland while making sure that I had the details right. I like getting the details right. It lets me sail and call it work . . . (That kettle is boiling. Just half a minute while I fill the teapot . . .) But I think you meant the country of the Swallows and Amazons. . . . In those four books, *Swallows and Amazons*, *Swallowdale*, *Winter Holiday* and *Pigeon Post*, the places are not given their proper names. But, in actual fact, I know that country better than any other. It is the country of my own childhood. In the case of the first book, I steered clear of using real names, for quite practical reasons. The place had to be disguised. So the Swallows and Amazons had a country of their own. Their lake is not altogether Windermere, though Rio is, of course, Bowness, because I had to take a good deal from Coniston. No island on Windermere has quite so good a harbour as that among the rocks at the south end of Peel Island on Coniston where I first landed from a little boat I hardly like to say how many years ago. And a good many people have spotted that Kanchenjunga must be the Old Man. But Cormorant Island is Silverholme on Windermere, and until a year or two ago the cormorants were there, and did a great deal of good by eating eels and thinning down the huge shoals of small perch. The perch one caught by that island were bigger in consequence. But now, alas, people have shot the cormorants and brought down the old dead tree on which they used to rest. Then, too, there had to be a little pulling about of rivers and roads, but every single place in all those books exists somewhere and, by now, I know the geography of the country in the books so well that when I walk about in actual fact, it sometimes seems to me that some giant or earthquake has been doing a little scene-shifting overnight.

Finally: as to how I began to write. I will tell you the truth, and let others take warning. I was not meant to be a writer at all. I was a cheerful small boy of action, very bad at lessons (as I remained) and with no thought of taking to a pen when, at about the age of eight, we were all

7

playing at ships under and on an old dining-room table, a really old one, with a heavy iron screw pointing downwards in the middle of it. It was my watch below when, suddenly, somebody else, who was on the bridge on the top of the table, raised a shout for 'All hands on deck!' I started up. That heavy iron screw made a horrible dent in the top of my skull, altering its shape and my character for life. I crawled out much shaken, played no more that day, but took a small blue notebook and wrote in it my first story, about a desert island. I have been at it ever since.

And now, Mr Woodfield, this letter has grown too long, and the tea is stewing. But you must allow me to send my very best wishes for the success of your *Junior Bookshelf* before signing myself

Yours sincerely,

ARTHUR RANSOME

1937

EVE GARNETT

The Family from One End Street, and Some of Their Adventures

illustrated by the author   FREDERICK MULLER

IN *Pigeon Post* the Library Association honoured the mature work of one who had been a pioneer of the modern children's book. The second Carnegie Medal went to a book which broke entirely new ground and which in twenty years has had few imitations and no equals. Eve Garnett found the material for *The Family from One End Street* in the streets and among the people of the little Sussex town in which she lived. She invented nothing, for there was to hand sufficient of drama and humour and pathos to make a hundred books. What she had to do, and she performed her task with the utmost skill and discretion, was to select characters who, without becoming types, would represent the everyday humours of working-class life.

Miss Garnett had two great qualifications: she was an artist, in line as well as words, of the highest integrity, and she felt strongly about children. (In 1938 her book of pictures *Is it well with the child?* made a powerful plea for social reform.) Out of love and anger, but principally love, she made her story of the Ruggles family who lived in One End Street. Mr Ruggles is a dustman, Mrs Ruggles takes in washing. They are blessed with a large family, and each chapter records the exploits of one member. Lily Rose helps her mother with the ironing, with disastrous results; Kate wins a scholarship and loses her school hat; the twins join a gang; and so on. In the last glorious chapter the whole family go to London for the Whitsun cart-horse parade. There are no great events; but the book shows beautifully the importance of small successes and failures to those sharing in them.

Since their first appearance the Ruggles family have enjoyed success in many countries. They are worthy emissaries, for they represent one aspect of English society most accurately, and usefully correct the impression given by the many stories of school life and of holiday adventure which make up the bulk of 'realistic' children's books. There is a very satisfying normality about the Ruggles. Their ambitions and their enterprises have a limited objective. They have common sense and a sense of responsibility. Above all, they are members of a family, and the book is one of the few which present an ordinary, happy and united family.

In 1937 *The Family from One End Street* was a topical book. It was a shot in the battle against slums. The battle has been largely won, but Miss Garnett's book has more than historic interest still, for it is concerned not merely with social problems but with human behaviour and human relationships. It remains one of the most entertaining and satisfying of all realistic books for children.

from Chapter X

'Why, I see our Jim down there,' said Mr Ruggles, 'that's his red head I'll swear – there – in that crowd by the Lake!'

'Here, take William!' cried Rosie, 'while I go and see – that's him all right,' she added, 'and there's Kate and there – ' she gasped – 'there's Peg – *with a Policeman* – oh, my goodness me!' and off she flew.

As Mrs Ruggles neared the crowd, Kate ran to meet her. 'Oo, Mum, come quick!' she cried, pulling her mother by the hand and stuttering in her excitement. 'P-Pamela's in the Lake and a p-policeman says our Peg's been s-stealing!'

'Oh, my goodness me!' cried Mrs Ruggles again, pushing her way into the crowd.

Sure enough, there was Peg, howling in the arms of a policeman, and Pamela, not in the Lake, but dripping on land and howling too, while Lily Rose and a Park-keeper did their best to wring the water out of her pink silk flounces!

'Whatever have you been doing of – are all the rest of you safe?'
cried poor Mrs Ruggles looking wildly round. Yes, there they all
were, the twins and Frankie Ruggles looking sheepish; Anthony, his
velvet suit torn and dusty, and his forehead decorated with a large
black bruise, swelling visibly; May and Doris, dirtier and untidier
than before, and Elfred, wet and muddy, but still grinning from ear
to ear. All there except Jo!

The Family from One End Street, pp. 145-6

EVE GARNETT was born in Worcestershire. She is the daughter of Lt-Col.
F. H. Garnett. She studied at the Royal Academy Schools, where she won
the Creswick Prize and Silver Medal. In her contribution to this book she
describes her first work leading to the writing of *The Family from One End
Street*. Her greatest interest is in painting, particularly murals (she did
mural decorations at Children's House, Bow). She lives in Sussex in the
'little town' of which she writes.

ONE REASON FOR 'ONE END STREET'

by EVE GARNETT

WHEN an art-student in London, more particularly at The Royal Academy
Schools whose premises are situated in the peculiarly airless basement of
Burlington House, I was unable for long at a time to stand the heat and
stuffiness of a Life School. I had come straight from the country – well
attested to by my very un-London-like shoes which, studded with nails, I
wore with complete unconcern until landed flat on my back on the
impeccable parquet of the National Gallery. I was for ever diving out for
air and, conscious-stricken that I was wasting time, would wander into
back streets and attempt to draw passers-by.

My knowledge of London was extremely slight, acquired in two or
three brief visits to relatives; little escorted tours – usually by the hand,
within the small radius of the West End. Of the East End I had heard – and
most certainly read, for to my neo-Georgian nursery had descended a
series of Victorian tales about The Poor. I had absorbed these tales very
thoroughly indeed, and for the East End, modified somewhat and consistent with the twentieth century, I was prepared. For what I was not
prepared were the slums into which I now wandered; streets not ten
minutes walk from my aunt's small, but eminently comfortable house in
South Kensington, or that of a more august relative in Sloane Street. The

time was the depression between the wars. Ex-service men and others stood bleakly patient at kerb-sides with trays of matches and shoe-laces; in the back streets wives and mothers stared despairingly into cheap food shops; and everywhere children swarmed – half-clothed, ill-fed, rickety. I began to explore farther afield but East, West, North or South the story was the same, and the impact on the spirit was shattering.

As time went on, burning with the zeal of propaganda, and also to augment my extremely small allowance from home, I one day approached a publisher with some of my back street drawings. The result was a commission to illustrate a book dealing with London children. Leave of absence from the R.A. Schools was granted and I put myself and my sketch-book at the disposal of the author who turned out to be no light task-master, demanding my presence at clinics, crèches, Council Schools, Nursery Schools, Play Centres, Children's Courts – and some of the worst slums from Deptford Docks to World End, Chelsea, at any hour from 7 a.m. to 7 p.m.

The book finished, I returned to the Schools but not long after its publication the great Trade Depression set in and I was haunted alike by social conditions and my inability to do anything about them through the only means available to me – illustrating. Every publisher was retrenching. Illustrated books, I was told, were definitely 'off' – 'except for children'.

'Except for children.' But social questions were for adults. But, were they – exclusively? I remembered my Victorian Tales. Glancing through contemporary children's bookshelves I could find nothing concerned with humans save sagas of the well-to-do. I thought again of my Victorians. Why should modern children not be presented with something on the same lines but in a less morbid and more humorous vein? But no author could be found to write such a book and at last, in sheer desperation, I decided to try and write one myself. *The Family from One End Street* was the result.

From the start its passage was stormy – (let those who yearn for Ivory Towers take heart!). Begun in the train visiting my mother in a Nursing Home, continued at intervals during her convalescence, and completed in the upheaval of a house-moving, it was consecutively rejected by six or more publishers, almost all, so far as I can remember, condemning it on the grounds of its total unsuitability for children. At last it was accepted – by John Lane Ltd. It was to have a delightful format, and 'profuse' illustrations. But alas, before it could be produced, the firm went into liquidation! Two more publishers turned it down, and it was finally accepted by the then-recently established firm of Frederick Muller, now under new management. An adequate but very different type of format was proposed, and the illustrations, to me the only enjoyable part of what had been hard and very uncongenial labour, few, and to be delivered within six weeks. The following week I went down with tonsilitis culminating in double quinsy; the majority of the illustrations were done in a kind of dazed convalescence, and remain – a lasting disappointment to the artist.

Whether the book ever succeeded, as propaganda, amongst children, is a moot point. Amongst adults – particularly adult males – judging from their letters, I think it may be said to have done so. But perhaps the, to me, most interesting feature in this direction was its selection in 1938 by the late Dr Goebbels for reading in German Schools, and, in 1946, by the Allied Commission for the same purpose!

I should like to end by saying that no one could wonder more than myself about the reason for the book's continuing appeal, both in English and translation; and that one of the nicest surprises it has brought me was to find it in a little shop in a war-scarred village far across the Arctic Circle in Northern Finmark. May it be that the poor, as we have been reminded, are with us always?

1938

NOEL STREATFEILD

The Circus is Coming
illustrated by Steven Spurrier   J. M. DENT

It is difficult to think of a time when Noel Streatfeild did not occupy her dominant position in the world of children's books, as the criterion of a particular kind of excellence. But in 1938 Miss Streatfeild was still relatively little known, although those children (and adults) who had read *Ballet Shoes* realized that here was a writer with her own brand of individual magic. *The Circus is Coming* confirmed the highest opinions, for here was a book which was gay, intelligent and highly individual.

Like all the best of Miss Streatfeild's books, *The Circus is Coming* is about work. 'Me, I don't understand bothering with anything unless you mean to work at it', says Ted Kenet. Miss Streatfeild understands idleness, but she is no more tolerant of it than Ted. Peter and Santa, in this book, are orphans brought up by a foolishly snobbish aunt, and left at her death with nothing but a totally unjustified sense of superiority. They run away from the threat of an orphanage to find their uncle who is tenting with Cob's Circus. In this fascinating setting they learn, painfully and slowly, how lacking they are in education and ability. At the end of the story two much nicer children are ready to become humble and useful members of their community.

A moral tale, in fact. But how gay, how free from priggishness is Miss Streatfeild's treatment of her serious subject. She effectively points the contrast between the orphans and the circus children, all of whom approach their work with the single-minded devotion of the professional. The little world of the circus is brought vividly to life, its colour and glamour and the hard work that lies behind every performance. The characters are clearly realized; not only obviously colourful individuals like the old Groom, but also more complicated characters like Uncle Gus. It is characteristic of Miss Streatfeild that the only characters who do not

14

ring true are the shallow unsympathetic people from Peter and Santa's world, and the story quickly turns its back on them.

The Circus is Coming is the result of hard thinking and hard writing. It represents the careful preparation, the rejection of easy solutions, which have made Miss Streatfeild one of the best loved but least prolific of writers.

Miss Streatfeild and Mr Steven Spurrier travelled with Bertram Mills' Circus to collect material for the book. Mr Spurrier fell ill before his finished drawings were ready, and the publishers issued the book with reproductions of the original sketches, full of swift and lively observation. In 1948 a new edition was prepared for which Mr Clark Hutton made a set of drawings in his characteristic style.

from Chapter VIII

The sea-lions were in their tank but there was a tremendous noise going on. Mr Schmidt was putting fish into a barrel. He smiled at Santa.

'My childrens are calling.' He patted the wagon. 'Each one to me is trying to say: "The band it plays. Do not be late".'

The poodles were behaving like a lot of ballerinas waiting in the wings for their entrances. Not for one second did they stay still. They wriggled. They stood on their hind legs. They shook themselves. Lucille, in her ring clothes and wig, was in with them. She held out her hand to Santa.

'Good evening.' She looked at her dogs with pride. 'They are great artistes, full of temperament.'

'They're awfully clever.' Santa agreed.

Lucille nodded.

'But difficult! You know how it is with artistes. Great children all of them. Some little thing is wrong, and they cannot give of their best. So I come down early and look at my dogs. How is it with you today, Simone? And you, Violette? Do you feel happy, Marie? And then I turn to Mis. She is my funny one. A little genius, that. And I say to her: "How are you, Mis?" I would like to say more. I would like to kiss her, but no.' She lowered her voice. 'All artistes are jealous. It is the temperament. If I kiss Mis, I must kiss them all, or they will not work.' *The Circus is Coming*, pp. 140–1

NOEL STREATFEILD is descended from a family of Kentish ironmasters, and, on her mother's side, from Elizabeth Fry. She was born in a Sussex vicarage. She was on the stage for a number of years, acting in Britain and the Dominions. Her first book was *The Whicharts*, an adult novel in which may be traced the seeds of *Ballet Shoes* which in 1936 marked her as an outstanding writer for children. Her books are equally popular and successful in the United States, and her critical writing in *Young Elizabethan* has considerable influence.

HOW 'THE CIRCUS IS COMING' CAME TO BE WRITTEN
by NOEL STREATFEILD

WHEN Miss Carey of Dent's asked me if I would write a book about the circus, I told her there was nothing I would like better, but that I only knew the circus from the spectator's angle, and would be quite incompetent to write a book about it. She said if I fancied writing the book, she thought she could arrange for me to study the subject, touring with Bertram Mills' Circus. Steven Spurrier, the artist, and his wife, would also be travelling with the circus, and he would illustrate the book.

Discovering the true life of a circus is a matter of patience; like most stage performers, circus people are self-centred, and it is hard to get them to talk about anybody but themselves. The great exception with the Mills' Circus was a wonderful old groom, who never mentioned himself, but talked of circuses generally, and particularly of his present and past horses.

All the other acts had to be learned about separately. When I wanted to know about lion taming I would sit and talk to the lady lion tamer. When it was the training of dogs I talked to the French woman who was in charge of performing poodles. When it was sea-lions I almost lived in the sea-lions' cage with the man who owned an extraordinarily clever troupe. If it was chimpanzees then I spent my time with the chimpanzee trainer. By far the best source for obtaining knowledge in a circus is from the clowns, who as a rule can perform in almost any act, and as well are frequently experienced tent hands.

I started the writing of *The Circus is Coming* during a seven weeks' voyage to America, and finished it in Los Angeles nine months later. A year later I was in the South of France writing a novel, when a telegram arrived, telling me that the book had won the Carnegie Gold Medal. I was going to the Cannes Casino that evening to dinner with Phillips Oppenheim, and I remember we celebrated the good news in champagne. Perhaps of all my children's books, I have most enjoyed writing *The Circus is Coming*, for it was such fun, even for a few weeks, feeling part of a circus.

1939

ELEANOR DOORLY

The Radium Woman: a youth edition of the life of Madame Curie
with woodcuts by Robert Gibbings   WILLIAM HEINEMANN

THE FIRST Carnegie Medals were awarded for works of fiction, and this was not surprising, not because of a lack of good factual books, but because the English genius in children's literature had from the beginning manifested itself most naturally in works of the imagination. *The Radium Woman* was outside the main tradition. What distinguished it in a year of good books was its quiet sincerity and humility, and the skill with which a great woman was brought to life.

In *The Radium Woman* Eleanor Doorly presented in a form acceptable to children the story told so movingly by Eve Curie in *Madame Curie*. Miss Doorly's book was, however, not merely a condensation of the larger work, but a re-creation of its theme and its spirit. It tells, in lucid prose, the life-story of Manya Sklodovska, who grew up under the tyranny of Russian overlordship in Poland, and who overcame incredible difficulties to satisfy her craving for learning, of her escape to Paris to work and work beyond normal human endurance and to find in Pierre Curie the perfect partner, of their great triumph, of Pierre's death in a trivial road accident and of her's at the hands of the Radium which she had discovered.

This is a great and inspiring story, and it is good that children should have access to it, particularly in a version which refrains from pointing morals or underlining sentiments. Miss Doorly had a great and enduring love of France, and this book has the restrained grace which is characteristic of French art. It is a remarkable achievement that the author, without any tricks of style, finds high drama in a story of scientific discovery. Marie Curie lived in an age of revolution, war and greed, but her life-story is one of a selfless quest for scientific truth. There is in this a worth-while lesson for children which is the more telling because it is implied

17

in every action of Marie's life but never stated in Miss Doorly's book.

Miss Doorly had in this, as in others of her books, the collaboration of Robert Gibbings, one of the finest of contemporary illustrators and perhaps the finest exponent of the craft of wood engraving. His decorations, whether of landscape or of homely domestic scenes, precisely match the grave unsensational tone of the story.

In a characteristic foreword Miss Doorly said that her object was to make her readers vow: 'We will not let ourselves be deprived of a word or a hint concerning that wonderful woman. We will also read Eve Curie's *Madame Curie*.' It was a modest aim. The experience of succeeding years has suggested that she was successful not only in sending readers to the larger work but also in giving them, at an impressionable age, an enduring image of the spirit of a great woman.

from Chapter XII

Marie and Pierre were sitting at home in the evening and Irène had been put to bed. That four-year-old tyrant had consented to shut her eyes and let Mé go back to Pierre to finish making the tyrant's dress, for Mé made all Irène's clothes. Suddenly Marie put down her work: 'Let's go back!' she said.

Pierre needed no asking. They had left their Radium only two hours but they longed to see it again. They wanted it as if it were a new baby. They called to Grandfather Curie that they were going out and then, arm-in-arm, through the crowded streets, past the factories of their unfashionable district, they made their way back to Rue Lhomond and their shed.

'Don't light up,' said Marie. 'Do you remember the day when you said you would like Radium to have a beautiful colour?'

In the dark of the shed, Radium had something even more lovely than colour. It had light!

'Look! look!' whispered Marie, as she felt her way to a chair and sat gazing round her.

There were tiny points of light in the dark room, like pale blue moonlight dancing on water, specks of light that were never still. On the table, on the shelves were those strange, mysterious radiances. In its little receptacles there was Radium visible at last, visible by its own light in the dark.   *The Radium Woman*, pp. 118–19

ELEANOR DOORLY died in 1950. The following impression has been written by Miss Winifred Fayerman, a distinguished educationist who was her lifelong friend.

ELEANOR DOORLY
by W. M. FAYERMAN

ELEANOR DOORLY was born in Jamaica; as a little girl, by then fatherless, she came to England, to the care of an elderly aunt in Leamington. The lanky, lonely child threw herself with avidity into the life and opportunities given her at Leamington High School, a smaller but equally progressive exponent of the pioneer work of Miss Buss and Miss Beale; for life she remained faithful to those of its staff and girls who won her heart, and rendered them many a kindness. Equipped with a London Degree in History and French, she acquired skill in teaching and a penetrating insight into the nature of youngsters at the North London Collegiate School, under its famous Headmistress, Mrs Bryant, for whom her reverence and admiration were unqualified. In due course she became a Headmistress, first of Twickenham County School for seven years, and then for twenty-two years of the King's High School, Warwick. In both these schools she went her own way, and it was an unconventional way; possessing a strong individuality herself, she also had a knack of inducing individuality in her girls; she despised shoddy work and loose conduct; the standard of scholarship, of self-reliance, and of social service in her school became high. Yet her influence and her effort were unobtrusive; her finger was always firmly on the reins, yet they were lightly held.

19

For she was always adding to her knowledge, and engaged on some personal work. She was a great traveller, unconventional, picking up the language and briefly sharing the lives of the people whose countries she visited; Norway, where she found an enduring family friendship; Ireland; the France that she so greatly loved. Although in her school days only a nodding acquaintance with science was given in girls' schools, she developed a keen interest in Natural History, and expressed it, and her understanding of children, both famously and delightfully, in her three books, *The Insect Man*, *The Microbe Man*, and *The Radium Woman*. Her vivid *Story of France* and *Ragamuffin King* are equally characteristic of her gifts; Henry of Navarre was a favourite hero. The warm humane spirit of the books shows through her beautiful, clear, simple English. An earlier book had been entitled *England in her Days of Peace*.

On her retirement in 1944, she went, in ill health, to live at Dartmouth, and died there in 1950.

Eleanor Doorly was a strange character; she was warmly valued both by many people of distinction, and by the less gifted; but some folks disliked her as much as others liked her. Was she an egotist, or a selfless lover of humanity? She seemed to be both. She was an introvert; for long a pacifist; a 'cat that walks by itself'; a lover of children; a social reformer; a staunch upholder of a genuine, not parasitic Christianity. She was generous to a fault, did much known good in the world, and there is no doubt that she did more that is unknown.

1940

KITTY BARNE

Visitors from London

with forty drawings by Ruth Gervis   J. M. DENT

THE WAR began in September 1939 with a gigantic picnic, the social experiment, comic, pathetic and occasionally tragic, of evacuation. The human problems springing from the removal of large numbers of people from their homes into an unfamiliar and often uncongenial setting provided rich material for the novelist. Among those who took up the challenge was Kitty Barne, and the Library Association awarded the fifth Carnegie Medal to a book which was thoroughly topical but which had the enduring qualities of universal humour and honest observation.

Visitors from London is a story of a family, the Farrars, of whom Miss Barne has written on several occasions. Four children, sensible, responsible but not priggish, they are on holiday with an aunt in Sussex, when the outbreak of war brings to them seventeen cockneys to be housed, fed and cared for. The story shows in a gay unsentimental fashion to what extent the visitors adapt themselves to country life and to one another. At the end of the story, Steadings, the old farm house, is empty once more. The experiment has failed; or has it? None of the visitors from London will ever be quite the same again. Each has learnt a little by an experience which has been more painful for some.

Miss Barne loves the country like a countrywoman; that is, she takes it for granted. Her descriptions are delightfully free of romanticism. The country for her, and for her characters, is a place to work in, and the most successful and happy of the evacuees is Fred who finds fulfilment and a satisfactory life among the Downland shepherds. Each of the characters is drawn with clean, bold lines. The difference between caricature and individual character-drawing is a fine one; but there is never any doubt about Miss Barne's skill. The 'visitors', like the residents, have an almost photographic realism. There are comic and pathetic episodes arising from the circumstances of evacuation, but the reader remembers most persistently, not events, but personalities; Lily, indomitable elder sister, Joe, who is determined to 'get on', Queenie, who considers Eastbourne 'chick', and above all Fred, who quickly decides that 'bein' in the country ain't 'arf a bit of all right'. Delightful three-dimensional characters all, who go on living outside the pages of the book. No wonder Miss Barne had to write a sequel!

R. Gorig.

from Chapter V

'I ain't sleepy,' Fred remarked scornfully. 'I don't never go to sleep before it's black. I could do with a look round.' He looked out of the window again, more wide awake than could be believed.

'But it is black, or very nearly,' said Myra firmly. 'You can't look round now. You'd wake all the animals up.'

'Animals? Is there animals? Wot, like the zoo?' Fred was incredulous.

'No, no, farm animals. Cows, pigs.'

'Can I see 'em?'

'Yes. Tomorrow. They'll all be there tomorrow, I promise you. Do go to bed now, for goodness' sake.'

'Right-oh, miss,' said Fred, and turned reluctantly away from the

window. 'It's a bit of all right, the country is. I never bin before.'
'You'll like it,' said Myra, and shut the door.

Visitors from London, p. 64

KITTY BARNE (Mrs Eric Streatfeild) is Noel Streatfeild's sister-in-law. Her books reflect a life-long love of music. She was trained at the Royal College of Music, and has been prominent in the musical activities of the Girl Guides Association. At the beginning of the war, as a member of the W.V.S. she found herself responsible for the reception of evacuees in Sussex, and *Visitors from London* was a result of this experience. Miss Barne suffered a stroke early in 1957, and was too ill to contribute to this volume. The following article is by her illustrator and sister-in-law, Mrs Ruth Gervis.

KITTY BARNE
as seen by her Illustrator – RUTH GERVIS

To an illustrator, Kitty Barne was a most delightful author, not because she gave one a free hand, far from it, but because she knew exactly what she wanted and was so delighted when one caught her visual images. Some authors just hand over the MSS and leave one to decorate their book, but with Kitty, it was a true collaboration of author and artist. After I had read over the MS, we would meet and then, her good ear towards me, her eyes shining, her face alive with interest, she would discuss her characters. I used to make dozens of quick sketches of every single character until I had got them as she pictured them, helped by her interjections, 'Oh, rather a higher forehead and even deeper set eyes' or 'Oh no, you've made her far too nice, I think she is a horrid little girl'. We would laugh together over her amusing adults as she suggested incidents for me to sketch which would bring out their characteristics.

To keep the children in character, I kept these sketch portraits by me while I was illustrating each book. I used to do roughs of a fair batch of illustrations and then send them off for her criticism – I think encouragement is the better word. Generally they would be as she wanted and her pleasure was spontaneous, but sometimes there would be a friendly protest such as a mother might make to a painter of her child's portrait. 'You've made her too old, she looks quite ten and she won't be nine till next birthday' or 'Aren't his legs too long and thin, he is a very sturdy boy'. She only saw the finished drawings after I had sent them to the publisher and then she used to write a long appreciative letter, going through nearly every drawing, and telling me which she liked best and why.

I think we both enjoyed doing *Visitors from London*. In those most unpleasant days it was a joy to be spending so much of one's time with imaginary people. My own recollections of doing the drawings are clear. We did everything as usual except that Kitty came to Sherborne instead of our usual meeting in London. We sent the rough sketches backwards and forwards, but because of the paper shortage we used always the same envelope and by the end it was so repaired and mended it was like a patchwork quilt. In this quiet, West County town, we had an early bomb or so and one bad raid. With three small children in the house, it was a rule to go to the shelter room whenever the siren sounded. All day I worked at the drawings and, at night, up to bed they went with me and down again they came to the shelter, at the far too frequent sirens; in fact the portfolio seemed to be my inseparable companion.

Another reason we both enjoyed this book so much was the setting; all the Sussex background was homeland to us both. We were reminded of far off peaceful days when prawns were caught and cooked at Birling Gap.

Eve Garnett

Noel Streatfeild

Kitty Barne

Mary Treadgold

D. J. Watkins-Pitchford (B.B.)   Eric Linklater

Elizabeth Goudge   Walter de la Mare

1941

MARY TREADGOLD

We Couldn't Leave Dinah

illustrated by S. Tresilian   JONATHAN CAPE

By 1940 the War had moved nearer. After the tragi-comedy of evacuation, the threat of invasion cast a shadow of potential tragedy over Britain. In July the Channel Islands fell to the enemy. Miss Mary Treadgold found in the transformation of a holiday island into an invasion base good material for a tale of adventure, which, for all that it made use of the traditional machinery of the thriller, was highly topical.

To the Templeton children, on holiday on the island of Clerinel, the war seemed remote; the activities of the Pony Club were of far more immediate interest. The news that 'Ole Hitler's goin' to take this island' brought Caroline's world crashing around her. After a breathless, and excitingly described, drive to the port, she and her brother are accidentally left behind on the quay just as the first airborne troops land. The two children make the cave in which the Pony Club have established headquarters into a temporary home, make contact with the Resistance and, after discovering some of the enemy's vital secrets, are taken off the island by destroyer.

We Couldn't Leave Dinah, more than any other Medal winning book, conforms to the conventional pattern of the adventure story. It has many of the essential elements: disguised conspirators, a secret hiding place, messages in code, nocturnal vigils, mistaken suspicions. It does however use these elements with exceptional skill. The timing is excellent. Suspense is held right up to breaking-point. No easy solutions, moreover, are found to the problems posed by the action of the story; Caroline and Mick have to earn success by their courage and intelligence.

Miss Treadgold used and developed a formula for the successful adventure story. She was also in *We Couldn't Leave Dinah* a pioneer of the Pony Book, a genre which became phenomenally popular in the immediate

C

post-war years. Dinah herself plays a relatively small part in the story, but ponies are essential to almost every crisis of the action. Readers will not readily forget the night ride which Caroline makes across the island on Punch 'like a fairy-tale ride through an enchanted country'.

Mr Stuart Tresilian's line drawings captured the atmosphere of some of the most exciting moments of the story. Still more they conveyed its freshness. It is essentially an open-air holiday story, for, however success-fully Caroline and Mick match their wits with the Nazis, they remain very ordinary children for whom invasion and the loss of their home are the occasion of a gloriously exciting picnic.

from Chapter XII

. . . Caroline yawned and slid into a full-length position in the radius of the warmth from the stove. The Cave was now deliciously fuggy. She stretched her arms out to their full length and rolled over and put her face down on them. She felt like a sleepy, purring little cat. Tonight, with its ride to Pol les Roches through the fog, seemed a long, long way off. Caroline relaxed every muscle in drowsy contentment. Dimly she heard Mick get up and draw the black-out curtain aside. 'What is it?' she murmured as a breath of cold air drifted across the warmth. But Mick had let the curtain fall again and had come back to his place.

'I only thought for a moment I heard an engine out in the bay,' he said. 'But there's nothing there. Isn't it beastly? But I think it'll lift before you have to go. Anyway, nothing very much can have happened since we saw Peter.'

'You're sure it wasn't Peter you heard?' Caroline sat up anxiously.

Mick shook his head. He looked at his watch. 'Five o'clock,' he said. 'If you leave about half-past eight you ought to do it nicely. No, there's nobody out in the bay. One always imagines one hears things in a fog.'

Five o'clock. The green hands of Mick's Luminex watch gleamed in the dark Cave. The children drew their rugs closer and settled down like Esquimaux in an igloo to wait for dark.

Out in the bay, with the fog muffling every sound, Peter chugged his engine backwards and forwards across the strip of ice-grey water, hoping against hope that its noise would penetrate the blanket of mist and convey his message to the children on the shore: 'Danger. Danger.'   *We Couldn't Leave Dinah*, pp. 192–3

MARY TREADGOLD was educated at St Paul's Girls School and at Bedford College, London. After a short time she entered publishing, first with Raphael Tuck's and afterwards as the first Children's Editor of Heinemann's. She explains how her experience in the work prompted her to write *We Couldn't Leave Dinah*. Her later work has included service with the B.B.C.

WE COULDN'T LEAVE DINAH

by MARY TREADGOLD

I find it very difficult across a span of nearly seventeen years to remember how a book, published when one seems to have been a different person, ever came to be written. I know all too well that it was written from no noble motive, and – in spite of a Swedish reviewer's admiration of 'Miss Treadgold's inspired Message' – contained, so far as I was aware, no noble purpose. I had been for a short while Children's Editor in a London publishing house, and through my hands had passed a staggering number of manuscripts about Ponies and Pony Clubs – a few, a very few, outstanding, the majority quite frightful – technically incompetent, at best derivative, at worst basely imitative. This was September, 1940, and, not being a knitter or caring for the sound of falling bombs, I occupied myself relatively painlessly in the air-raid shelter with trying to implement my own verdict, 'I could do it better myself!'

The plot derived, of course, immediately from the news that summer of the invasion of the Channel Islands. In a passion of recollection, I thought of those islands as I had known them in childhood. I recalled the warm, sunlit lanes, the sudden sharp glimpses of the sea, and the tiny harbours hidden among the cliffs, and, in the unhealthy atmosphere of the shelter, transmuted all to what, even in childhood memory, they had never quite been – islands of the blest, with woods undisturbed by world-horror through which the children ran, and with thyme-scented uplands and shining sands across which they rode. In that way nerves were steadied, and a peace unsteadily, inconstantly, but occasionally evoked.

The ponies themselves, their names, their personalities, and the way they were ridden and managed belonged to a later phase of schooldays – to Easter holidays on Dartmoor when I clattered around, and up and down and over things, on a phlegmatic little pony with a mouth of iron. The children themselves – Mick and Caroline – were quite simply the kind that at fourteen I would like to have been myself: extrovert, with clear-cut and developed values, plenty of courage, and good at games – I having been the kind of child who had and was none of these things. So, as I remember it now, it looks as if the whole of *We Couldn't Leave Dinah* was a mixture of escape and wish-fulfilment, motivated by a robust and scornful competitive sense – and indeed I think there are worse reasons for writing a book, though many better. If anything extra got into the book – anything in the way of pity and courage that has never appeared in other more recent books that I have had published – it was, I think,

28

because it was written in a time when to be a Londoner was to look gladly out from the windows of a fortress and to find that along with everybody else, one had for a little while become far-sighted . . .

I was shaken at the book being awarded the Carnegie Medal – and I still am. If I were a Children's Editor now I would find it a readable book, competent, and, I hope, likeable. But I would find it an example of the way in which a popular book can be confused with one of a high level of achievement – and I would not feel hurt if it were remembered as such among all the other books that have been awarded the Medal. I used to wonder at the time, I remember, what quiet book, what book with a less obviously popular appeal was overlooked that year . . .

1942

'BB'

The Little Grey Men: a story for the young in heart
illustrated by Denys Watkins-Pitchford   EYRE AND SPOTTISWOODE

AFTER two topical stories, a timeless one. 'BB' found a constant factor
in a changing world in the pattern of the seasons and in the light, colour
and movement of a Midland stream. As a life-long naturalist and sportsman, he knew intimately the details of life among small wild creatures and
could share in their experiences. He chose to write about gnomes, but
The Little Grey Men is not a fantasy. It is a consistent picture of the natural
world. There is no magic in it. Even the destruction of Giant Grum (the
gamekeeper) is accomplished not by the intervention of Pan but by the
application of a piece of sportsman's lore.

The Little Grey Men is a tale of the last gnomes in England, who leave
the shelter of their oak-tree home to voyage upstream in search of their
missing brother, Cloudberry. Their names are Sneezewort, Baldmoney
and Dodder. They are 'honest-to-goodness gnomes, none of your baby,
fairy-book tinsel stuff, and they live by hunting and fishing'. They are
very small and are able to share the life of woodland birds and beasts, at
peace with most of them, but living in dread of such carnivores as fox and
stoat. They journey first in *Dragonfly*, an ingenious home-made paddle-
boat, then on foot, and lastly in the *Jeanie Deans*, a brand-new clockwork
steamer which an unfortunate child lost on its maiden voyage.

The peculiar charm of *The Little Grey Men* is that it is written to scale.
'BB' has managed to forget his stature and to see the world as if from a
height of a few inches. The setting is most beautifully realized, and the
story is pervaded with the sound of flowing water, water which is sometimes an ally, sometimes an enemy, but omnipresent. It is an exciting
story but the excitement springs from the natural hazards of the journey.
There are no invented, spurious thrills. 'BB' has appended to his story the
motto:

'The wonder of the world, the beauty and the power,
the shape of things,
their colours, lights, and shades; these I saw.
Look ye also while life lasts.'

He successfully opens his readers' eyes and helps them to see for themselves the beauty of the English countryside.

The author of *The Little Grey Men* is his own illustrator, and successive editions reflect his changing technique. The original edition was decorated most liberally with scraperboard drawings, twenty-one of which were full-page. Every chapter had head and tail-pieces and decorative initials. Within the limits of the medium, these illustrations were extraordinarily successful in evoking the open-air spirit of the story. In 1946, in a new edition, most of the original pictures were eliminated and instead eight reproductions of oil-paintings were included. These, admirable in original, suffered badly in reproduction. A new edition in 1952 discarded all these coloured pictures (except one used – not very successfully – on the dust-jacket), brought back six of the original large scraper-boards, and introduced a new frontispiece in line and colour. On comparing the three editions it is difficult to come to any other conclusion than that the first is easily the most satisfactory in format and in harmony of text and illustration.

from Chapter XVIII

They broke the thin film of ice round the ship with oars and after much hauling and pushing they got the nose of the *Jeanie Deans* round. A moment later the current took her and, free of ice, she began to drift as silently as a fallen leaf downstream. . . .

The gnomes went back down the Folly with a great company. Each tree as they passed it flung some dead leaves down to them, the stream was full; hawthorn, maple, chestnut, elm, oak, lime, willow, ash, and alder, poplar and wild apple, all were drifting with the current, smoothly and silently, in a coloured carpet.

There was nothing to do all day but stand about the deck, smoke and gossip, admire the scenery, and lean over the side to watch the endless procession of coloured leaves sliding past, to watch the darting fish in the clear water, and wave to astonished watervoles.

It is a strange thing that before the floods in late autumn, rivers, streams, and ponds become crystal clear.

It was possible for the gnomes to see every pebble and leaf on the stream bed, and the waving cresses, some like green hair, and neat

pillows of tight, green weeds, seemed to belong to a fantastic sub-
marine fairyland.   *The Little Grey Men*, pp. 245–6

'BB' (D. J. Watkins-Pitchford) was trained at the Schools of Painting and
Engraving of the Royal College of Art, in the former under Sir William
Rothenstein. He taught art at Rugby School. 'BB' is well known as a
writer on country life and sports and as an illustrator, particularly in
black-and-white. He lives in the Northamptonshire countryside of which
he writes in *The Little Grey Men*.

THE LITTLE GREY MEN
by 'BB'

THE story of how *The Little Grey Men* was first born in my mind
begins on a bright Easter Monday, somewhere in the nineteen-
twenties. With my twin brother I walked up the brook which
flowed below our old home in Northamptonshire, a tributary
of the Nene, a small brook rush-grown in places, bushed in by hawthorns,
with many a bend and miniature beach. The rooks cawed above their
still-visible nests in the field-elms and we talked with the signalman, I
remember, as he leant on the rails of his box by the level crossing at
Draughton.

Funny how one remembers these things: the delicious gentle warmth
of the spring sunshine, the sparkle of the stream, the celandines bright and
varnished, the scent of wild water mint.

We had set out to find the source of this brook. We never went far
enough, we had to turn back in the early afternoon. In any case, the
stream had quite lost its magic, it was then merely a half-hidden ditch
crossing tussocky fields.

It was on those sudden secret shingles, at a bend in the stream where an
old oak arched over, I thought of *The Little Grey Men*. The idea lay
dormant for over twenty years until I was teaching at Rugby School and
had the time to write the story.

The Folly Brook is not changed at all. I visited it only the other day.
There is a new concrete monstrosity which replaces the old ivy-clad bridge
by Lamport station, but the bright waters still thread the meadows up to
Maidwell and Draughton and, on a spring morning, descendants of those

rooks I heard cawing in the rookery are still vociferous in the gentle April days.

Without those vivid recollections I could never have written *The Little Grey Men*; there was no need to invent a setting, it was there, in my mind, every meadow, every bend, every bush and tree, though the Clobber Park in the story is another locality in an adjacent county which, with artistic licence, I moved into Northamptonshire.

As a boy I believed with Llewelyn Powys that if 'I could become invisible and be transported to the tall elder hedge across the field, or in a trice, to be on the other side of the green hill where the red-legged moorhen has her nest amid the basket rushes of the ox pond', I would surprise the little people about their business.

And in the magic white twilights of new summer I still get that feeling. When it fades I shall no longer write books for children.

1944

ERIC LINKLATER

The Wind on the Moon: a story for children
Nicolas Bentley drew the pictures MACMILLAN

THE first awards had gone to writers who, even if they worked in a variety of forms, were primarily known in the field of children's literature. In 1944 the Library Association caught a literary lion. Eric Linklater had won high distinction as novelist, poet, dramatist and biographer. He was, moreover, a man of affairs and of action. To children's books he brought exuberance, a strong sense of character and narrative, virtuosity in the use of words, and a Gargantuan sense of humour.

The Wind on the Moon is the story of two little girls, Dinah and Dorinda, children of character whose high spirits, courage and determination lead them, not unnaturally, into naughtiness. There was a wind on the moon on the night that father went away, and it blew straight into their hearts, making them behave badly for a year. In this time they over-ate until they looked and rolled like balloons, and turned into kangaroos and joined a zoo. This, surprisingly, was the beginning of their reformation, and the story concludes with their successful mission, in human shape but accompanied by two animals from the zoo, to rescue their father from a dictator's prison in middle-Europe. But summary makes nonsense of a story full of gay invention, good humour and suspense. It is a long story but it has no longueurs.

The Wind on the Moon is a comic fantasy and, like the best of this kind, is both serious and deeply concerned with reality. It is certainly rich in comic situations and characters, and some of the latter – Mr Parker, the detective-giraffe, Bendigo the bear who reads *The Times*, Miss Serendip the omniscient governess – are among the memorable inventions of recent years. Some of the nonsense has an adult tone, playing lightly with purely adult ideas and experiences; the same is true of Lewis Carroll, and children like both for the wayward eloquence of their expression. The whole story is touched with seriousness, however; and the sober mood gains ascendancy as the children set out on their hazardous journey to Bombardy. The final episodes, particularly the death of the Golden Puma, are described with fine restraint. Even here humour breaks through. The *dei ex machina* who rescue Major Palfrey and his daughters are two sappers left over from the Crimean War.

All this is in the full stream of the English nonsense tradition, but it is not just nonsense spun for a child's amusement. It is firmly based on sound observation and thinking. Mr Linklater was writing in wartime, and did not forget that there were tyrants more brutal than County Hulagu Bloot, and that others besides the Golden Puma had died for their friends. *The Wind on the Moon*, for all its effortless gaiety, had deeper undertones.

The book was a remarkably good example of wartime production, and the illustrations, by Nicolas Bentley, captured the grave gaiety of the story in most satisfying fashion.

from Chapter IX

'Weren't you a giraffe when you were born?' asked Dinah.

'Indeed I wasn't,' said Mr Parker indignantly. 'I was one of the most beautiful babies in England. I took first prize at a Baby Show! Then I grew up and became a detective. I was one of the best detectives in the world. I used to capture murderers by the dozen, forgers by the score, and hundreds of burglars. But one day when I was trying to look over a very high wall – craning up and up, stretching my legs and stretching my neck – a strange thing happened. Suddenly I found that I could see over it quite easily. I had become enormously tall! And there, on the other side of the wall, there was a burglar burying a lot of silver plate in a flower-bed. 'I arrest you!' I shouted, but my voice sounded strange, and when the burglar looked up he uttered an exclamation of intense surprise.

You had become a giraffe,' said Dinah.

'I had,' said Mr Parker sadly.

'What happened then?' asked Dorinda.

'The burglar, who was a bold and quick-witted man, came out and stroked me,' said Mr Parker. 'I was quite astonished, because, as probably you know, it is most unusual for a detective to be stroked by a burglar. I moved slightly away from him, and happened, at the same moment, to catch sight of my legs. I looked round and saw my back. I was bewildered by the change in my appearance, and the burglar, taking advantage of my perplexity, led me away and finally sold me to Sir Lankester Lemon for fifty pounds.'

'It must have been magic that turned you into a giraffe,' said Dinah.

'I don't believe in magic,' said Mr Parker stubbornly.

'Then how did it happen?' asked Dorinda.

'I don't know,' said Mr Parker, 'but people often get what they want, if they want it long enough. Think of all the people who say, "All I want is peace and quiet". And sooner or later they die, and what could be quieter than that? And I, you see, had always wanted to look over walls.' *The Wind on the Moon*, pp. 82-4

ERIC LINKLATER was born in 1889. He was educated at Aberdeen Grammar School, and served in the First World War in the Black Watch. He studied medicine and then English at Aberdeen University, and became first a journalist in India, then a lecturer in the University. He stood, unsuccessfully, as a Scottish Nationalist candidate in a by-election. In the Second World War he served in Orkney and at the War Office. He has travelled widely in America, the Far East and Australasia. In 1954 he was awarded the C.B.E.

THE WIND ON THE MOON
by ERIC LINKLATER

It is said that Indian music – perhaps all primitive music? – was strictly functional: designed, that is, to fulfil a given purpose. There were, for example, tunes to make young women fall in love; tunes to raise fire, and other tunes to put it out.

In this respect, *The Wind on the Moon* is remarkably similar to primitive music; for in its simple, original form it was entirely purposive. It was designed – and told at the top of my voice – to drown the loud, ill-tempered howling of my two small, rain-soaked daughters.

The year, I think, was 1941, and I had come home for a few days' leave after a mission to Iceland and the Faroes. I had been in uniform since the outbreak of war, and after eighteen months of relatively honest but highly incompetent service in command of a sapper company in the Scapa Flow defences had been removed to employment, of much greater interest but perhaps of less merit, under the War Office. But I was in uniform; that is the point I want to make.

The children were six and eight years old, or thereabout; and, like all small girls, self-centred. They enjoyed their leisure, they hated to be

37

disturbed. And one day, when my wife instructed me to take them for a walk, we all protested; for I was sure it was going to rain, and they disliked exercise in any circumstances. But we had been told to go for a walk and, after some unavailing argument, we went. Obedient, but unwilling, and the two children openly rebellious.

We were living, temporarily, in the Eastern Borders; in the village of St Boswell's. Our home, at that time, was in Orkney, but for some reason or other – there was fear of German invasion, or German raiding of the islands – my family had been evacuated; and my wife had omitted to bring any clothes for me. Plain clothes, that is. So I was still in uniform when I took the children walking, and that was ridiculous for a start.

We walked up-hill, across country, and they fell into ditches, or scratched themselves on gorse and briars. They made no pretence of enjoying themselves, and when it began to rain they proclaimed their dissatisfaction with appalling vigour. We turned towards home, and took the nearest route; which lay along a public road. The children howled continuously, and passers-by stared curiously. I was in uniform, I repeat, and to passers-by I was obviously the embodiment of military sadism; of which they had heard so much.

The situation was manifestly intolerable and to cure it I began to tell a story. I told it very loudly, shouting down the anger of the children – and presently won their attention. I continued my story, desperately improvising to prevent renewal of their wrath, and when we got home we were all very wet, but comparatively happy. And that was the genesis of *The Wind on the Moon*.

1946

ELIZABETH GOUDGE

The Little White Horse

illustrated by C. Walter Hodges   UNIVERSITY OF LONDON PRESS

THE next book to receive a Medal was also a fantasy, but there could be no greater contrast than that between Mr Linklater's exuberant fancy and Miss Goudge's poetical morality. Elizabeth Goudge was a firmly established novelist in 1946, with several books, one of which had enjoyed a phenomenal success, already to her credit. Her particular qualifications for the writing of books for children were warmth and sincerity. She clearly loved children as much as she loved goodness, but always without mawkishness.

In *The Little White Horse* Miss Goudge wrote a book which in many ways harked back to the previous century. Her master, if she had one, was George Macdonald. *The Little White Horse* is a 'moral tale', an allegory, in which an acceptable lesson is carried through the medium of an enchanting story. Children, who in any case are less averse to a moral than their elders, have shown no wish to complain that this story, with its excitement, its vividly realized setting, and its many colourful characters, is concerned with the nature of good and evil and with the importance of self-discipline. It is in fact, in the strictest sense, a *good* book.

Of the many delightful elements in *The Little White Horse* the most immediately, and lastingly, agreeable are setting and character. It is a Devon story. The landscape is perhaps idealized, but it is described with loving accuracy. The reader becomes intimately acquainted with the charms of Moonacre, the manor house and park, and the adjacent village of Silverydew overshadowed by Paradise Hill. In the creation of character, one recognizes the skill of a professional writer. Each of the charming and odd people who live in this enchanted valley is seen clearly. The fantasy is anchored firmly by characters who, if they are painted somewhat larger and more colourfully than life, have an imaginative reality of their own.

Richard Armstrong

Agnes Allen

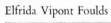

Cynthia Harnett

Mary Norton

Edward Osmond

Ronald Felton (Ronald Welch)

C. S. Lewis

The little heroine, Maria, is particularly well done, a most skilful blending of strength and weakness, whose genuine sweetness is seasoned with a drop of acid.

The charms of character and scene are captured once and for all by Mr C. Walter Hodges' illustrations in line and colour. It would be impossible to imagine any other interpreter. Much as he loves the grotesque, he keeps his drawings well on the right side of caricature, and retains the reader's sympathies for them, for this is a book in which the reader is called upon to side with all the characters, good and bad.

One of the tests of a good book is the degree to which the reader enters into the life of the characters. One shares, in an intensely personal way, in the fortunes of Maria as she sets about her tasks of bringing back harmony, after many centuries, to Moonacre Manor and the village of Silverydew.

from Chapter III

'Now then, good people of Silverydew,' he cried, his flashing eyes passing over the packed congregation, 'with all your hearts and souls and voices sing praises.' Then he raised his head and glanced at the choir in the gallery. 'And you up there, keep in tune for the love of God.'

Then he suddenly whisked up a fiddle from somewhere inside the pulpit, tucked it under his chin, raised his right arm with the bow clasped in his thin brown fingers, brought it down upon the strings with superb artistry, and swung his people into the winging splendour of the Old Hundredth with something of the dash and fire of a cavalry officer leading his men to the charge.

What a row! Up in the gallery the fiddlers and the 'cellists and Digweed played like men possessed. Though she could not see them, Maria could picture their red perspiring faces and their arms sawing back and forth, and their shining eyes almost popping out of their heads with eagerness and joy. And every man and woman and child in the congregation was singing at the top of his or her voice. Maria herself sang till her throat ached, with Sir Benjamin upon one side of her bellowing like a foghorn and Miss Heliotrope upon the other trilling like a nightingale. Miss Heliotrope's trilling astonished Maria. She had never heard Miss Heliotrope trill before. She hadn't even known she could trill. And it seemed to Maria, her imagination running riot to a shocking extent, that beyond the walls of the church she could hear all the birds in the valley singing, and the flowers singing, and the sheep and deer and rabbits singing in the park and woods and fields and up on the slopes of the great hills. And somewhere the waves of the sea that she had not seen yet were rolling into Merryweather Bay, and crying Amen as they broke upon the shore. And up there in the tall pulpit stood the Parson playing the fiddle as Maria had never heard a fiddle played before, and never would again, because no one in all the world ever had, or ever would, play the fiddle as superbly as the Parson of Silverydew.

The Little White Horse, pp 66–7 ·

'Singing Praises'

42

ELIZABETH GOUDGE's novels provide a commentary on her life. *A City of Bells* describes Wells where she was born and where her father was Principal of the Theological College. *Island Magic* is a story of Guernsey, from which her mother came and where she spent her childhood holidays. *Towers in the Mist* is a story of Christ Church where she lived from 1923, when her father became Regius Professor of Divinity at Oxford. *The Little White Horse* is set in Devonshire, where she went to live on her father's death in 1939. She lives now near Henley-upon-Thames.

THE LITTLE WHITE HORSE

by ELIZABETH GOUDGE

I have always been fascinated by the unicorn. This blue-eyed, snow-white beast, with the white horn tipped with scarlet, whose mysterious form passes in and out of the pages of the Old Testament, fights the Lion for the Crown in the old nursery rhyme, and faces him above it in the Arms of England, who is he and where does he come from? Centuries ago there were folk who claimed to have seen the silvery figure cantering noise-lessly by in the woods, behind the stems of the trees, but they were always alone when they saw him and their evidence was without support. The unicorn has always been a shy beast, keeping both his distance and his secret. When before the last war I lived in Oxfordshire and visited Ewelme Church, where the effigy of Thomas Chaucer, the son of the poet and Warden of the Chiltern Hundreds, lies in state upon his tomb, I was excited to find that Thomas's feet rested upon a unicorn and I wondered if Thomas had ever seen one in the Chiltern beechwoods. When a few years later I went to live in a cottage in Devonshire, I was even more excited to see that the weather-vane upon the old farmhouse we saw from our windows was a small white figure with a flowing mane and tail. Closer inspection revealed him to be not a unicorn but a little white horse, yet when I watched him prancing in the west wind from the moors, or swinging round, heading away from the east wind from the sea, I always seemed to see a horn entangled in his mane. For years he was the first thing I looked at when I drew the curtains away from the kitchen window in the morning, and very soon he became so important to me that I began to weave a story around him. Those were the war years and it was good to escape sometimes from the fearful realities of that time into a world where a unicorn cantered behind the trees. If I had thought the Chiltern beech-woods a suitable habitat for unicorns, I thought the round green hills, the woods and warm valleys of South Devon even more suitable. For Devon is enchanted country when the tourists are away. Anything may happen there, and a great deal does happen of a mysterious nature, about which Devon people do not talk a great deal to the outsider. The landscape of my story was ready for me. Behind the little white horse swinging in the wind the long green slopes of Paradise Hill climbed the sky. Westward in the deep woods a ruined Norman castle reared itself up upon the rock. It was a haunted place and I never wanted to be there alone. There was no doubt that Black Men lived there. The Church with its ancient peal of bells was the church I went to, and Moonacre Manor was not far from the Church. In the lane outside our cottage there was a steep bank covered with periwinkle, that country people call joy-of-the-ground. In the writing of the book there was no need to invent the landscape but only to people it. The landscape was all there.

Now it is largely covered with bricks and mortar and I am back again in Oxfordshire, in the Chiltern country of Thomas Chaucer's unicorn. I heard cantering hoofs one night, in the field outside my window, and when I looked out I saw a little white horse flashing by in the moonlight. The fire of a gypsy encampment was glowing in the hollow below the field. He might have been a gypsy pony, or again he might not.

1947

WALTER DE LA MARE

Collected Stories for Children

illustrated by Irene Hawkins FABER AND FABER

WALTER DE LA MARE'S *Collected Stories for Children* was a new book of 1947 in a bibliographical, not a literary sense. Each of the seventeen tales had been printed before, one as long ago as 1900. The publication of the *Collected Stories* offered, however, the last opportunity for the Library Association to recognize the unique contribution which Walter de la Mare had made to children's literature. For nearly half a century he had devoted to children the same qualities which had made him so distinctive and memorable a writer of prose and verse for adults. No other writer had given so generously of his best to children, so that it was impossible to say that *Peacock Pie* was inferior to *Motley* or *The Three Mulla-Mulgars* to *The Return*. It was therefore a cause for rejoicing that the Library Association had interpreted in so liberal a spirit its regulations by honouring a book which so richly summed up a life devoted to the delight and the under-standing of children (for although Walter de la Mare had nine more years before him, he wrote no more for children).

With one exception all the stories in this collected edition had been published before in *Broomsticks and Other Tales* (1925) and *The Lord Fish* (1933), two volumes of an exceptional beauty, illustrated respectively by Bold and Rex Whistler. They had also appeared in four volumes, with the present illustrations, between 1942 and 1946. Several had made their first appearance in *Joy Street*, most delightful of annuals, and some had been included in other collections, such as *Seven Short Stories* (1931) adorned by John Nash in characteristic style. One, *The Old Lion*, had been published separately in a particularly pleasant form as *Mr Bumps and His Monkey* (1942) with memorable drawings by Dorothy P. Lathrop.

Collected Stories for Children is representative of the creative work of forty years. It has, nevertheless, a remarkable unity in mood and style, however

45

diverse the subject-matter and the treatment. Some of the stories are perhaps *of* rather than *for* children. *Maria-Fly*, for example, demands more self-contemplation than a child will normally be prepared to give, although it enters the absorbed, practical world of the child with confidence. 'If there was one thing Maria couldn't abide, it was a fly floating in her bath. It was extraordinary that though its carcase was such a minute thing you could at such a moment see absolutely nothing else. It was extraordinary that the whole of the water at such a moment seemed like fly water.' This is no adult's interpreting the child's vision from outside. The best of the stories, however, are definitely for children. For all his leisurely manner, and the richness with which he adorns and develops each idea, he is a fine and persuasive narrator. He buttonholes his young audience like a genial Ancient Mariner. In such a story as *The Lord Fish* the digressions, the confidential asides, the poetical and colloquial imagery, all maintain the impression of an exceptionally gifted ballad-man with an art that closely resembles spontaneity. Walter de la Mare is always a poet, but his poetry is as natural as air. Here is Jasper, the regal monkey of *The Old Lion*: 'Jasper . . . was quiet as flowing water and delicate as the flowers beside it. When he touched, it was as if thistledown had settled at his finger-tips. When he stretched out his fingers to take an apple, it was like the movement of a shadow through the air.'

Whether he is telling a straightforward but characteristic tale like *Dick and the Beanstalk*, touching the heart with the bitter-sweet *Three Sleeping Boys of Warwickshire*, chilling the spine with *The Riddle*, Walter de la Mare is in all these stories a fine craftsman and a sensitive observer. He never condescends to his readers, and never forgets that, of all the wonders in the world which he explores so profoundly and so sadly, the greatest wonder is the child's fresh and penetrating vision. 'I know well,' he says in *Bells and Grass*, 'that only the rarest kind of best in anything can be good enough for the young.' That was the guiding principle in his own writing for children. It may well be the yardstick by which aspirants to a Carnegie Medal are measured.

from *Dick and the Beanstalk*

These tales not only stayed in Dick's head, but *lived* there. He not only remembered them, but thought about them; and he sometimes dreamed about them. He not only knew almost by heart what they told, but would please himself by fancying what else had happened to the people in them after the tales were over or before they had begun. He could not only find his way about in a story-book, chapter by chapter, page by page, but if it told only about the inside of a house he would begin to wonder what its garden was like – and in imagination would find his way out into it and then perhaps try to explore even further. It was in this way, for example, that Dick had come to his own conclusions on which finger Aladdin wore his ring, and the colour of his uncle the Magician's eyes; on what too at last had happened to the old Fairy Woman in *The Sleeping Beauty*. After, that is, she had ridden off on her white ass into the forest when the magic spindle had begun to spread the deathly slumber over her enemies that was not to be broken for a hundred years. *He* knew why she didn't afterwards come to the Wedding!

And as for Blue-beard's stone-turreted and many-windowed castle, with its chestnut gallery to the east, and its muddy moat, with its carp, under the cypresses, Dick knew a good deal more about *that* than ever Fatima did! So again, if he found out that Old Mother Hubbard had a *cat*, he could tell you the cat's name. And he could describe the crown that Molly Whuppie was crowned with when she became Queen, even to its last emerald. He was what is called a *lively* reader.   *Collected Stories for Children*, pp. 9–10

WALTER DE LA MARE was born in Charlton, Kent, in 1873. Of Huguenot stock, he was descended on his mother's side from Browning. He was educated at St Paul's Choir School and worked for eighteen years in the Anglo-American Oil Company. He retired with a small Civil List pension at the age of thirty-five. He was made a Companion of Honour in 1948 and appointed to the Order of Merit in 1953. He died in 1956. *Songs of Childhood*, in 1902, his first book, marked him as the most original of all writers of poetry for children. Equally distinguished in poetry, the short story and criticism, he made a unique contribution to literature in a number of long discursive anthologies.

The following memories are recorded by Eleanor Farjeon, his friend for forty years.

REMEMBERING WALTER DE LA MARE

by ELEANOR FARJEON

I have told somewhere else how, in 1913, Edward Thomas handed me one of his two review copies of a new book of poems, saying, 'Read this, and if you are worthy of it, keep it.' The name of the author was unknown to me. The name of the book was *Peacock Pie*. Needless to say, I kept it.

Three years later Edward took me to see Walter de la Mare in his old-fashioned house in Anerley. That autumn afternoon began the friendship that was like a slow-flowing river over forty years, stealing unsuspected from its source, gathering impetus as it neared the sea. Before we met again the war had come to an end, and my life as a writer began in earnest. When *Tunes of a Penny Piper* and *Songs for Music* were published, W.J. asked for poems from my 'two little honeypots' for his anthologies. Soon occasions arose when we went together to Girls' Schools and Children's Libraries, he to read his poems and I to sing my Nursery Rhymes. His presence gave me confidence, for I was always shy of appearing on a platform for any reason, and, oddly enough, I felt that he liked support almost as much as I needed it. Once, when I had written describing a prize-giving I had braced myself to attend alone, he wished, in his reply, that he had been there 'disguised as a little creature with blue ribbons in her hair and a muslin frock'; and in turn described one of his recent prize-givings at a girls' school – 'and it was awful to feel the smile from the heart steadily stiffening into the plaster of Paris of habit – and *yet* to be coming from the same place, I believe.'

But we enjoyed to the hilt our shared occasions at a remarkable L.C.C. 'Infant and Juniors Mixed' school in Bethnal Green, some of whose six hundred pupils came to their classes almost shoeless and in rags. The head-mistress, Mrs Mary Dean, had fired her staff, and so the children, with her passion for imaginative education, and had divided her pupils into four houses, named Rudyard Kipling, Laurence Housman, Walter de la Mare, and Eleanor Farjeon. Each house had its flag and colours, and a motto from its own author. W.J. had already acceded to the request which Mary Dean urged in her first letter to me: 'Do come and let the children see and *touch* you, and know you are *real*.' I went – was seen – and was touched, in a deeper sense than one. After this W.J. and I joined forces at the Christmas Parties, superbly organized in a huge gymnasium by Mary, her staff, and an energetic Vicar. At one of these parties the children were in fancy dress, and we were to judge the prize-winning costumes. 'My word, it's going to be very hard,' he whispered, taking notes as the children paraded round and round the hall, to some raucous mechanical music ground out by the Vicar. We gave the go-by to the Pierrettes and Toreadors hired from the costumiers by the better-off mothers, and the Boys' Prize went to a small youth rigged up in newspapers, calling himself 'Late Final', and the Girls' to a little Charwoman, decked in her mother's dishcloths and dusters. Then the Captain of Farjeon House dashed up to drag me into the dance – a Valeta, which I didn't know, but it seemed not to matter; and W.J. sat laughing each time I whirled by with another hairpin fallen out. It may have been with the recollection of that pre-War party that he wrote to me in 1950: 'I am so glad you had that very lively Christmas; but then, you see, by a freak of Destiny wheresoever you happened to be (even on the slopes of Etna) couldn't but be a lively Christmas.'

1948

RICHARD ARMSTRONG

Sea Change

with line drawings by M. Leszczynski   J. M. DENT

Sea Change was the first boys' book to receive the Carnegie Medal. It was also one of the first, and remains the best, of career books for boys. It was born of a desire not only to tell a fine tale but also to help boys through the difficult process of growing up.

Cam, the hero of *Sea Change*, is an apprentice in the Merchant Navy. Sailing on his third voyage, he is a keen, tough, likeable lad with a very large chip on his shoulder. He is anxious to learn his job quickly and is impatient with the many tedious routine chores on shipboard. During the voyage he discovers, by trial and error, that he is in fact mastering his craft and that the mate who seemed to be perversely thwarting him has known exactly what he is doing.

There is much action in the story – a clash with the military, a fire at sea, and, as a climax, the salvaging of a derelict ship – but the incidents, though described with authority, are conventional. The great interest of *Sea Change* derives from Mr Armstrong's intense and passionate concern with the seaman's job. He describes each process simply but with a full understanding of its purpose; and he is deeply interested in the ways in which a man grows and is moulded by the work he does.

It is his achievement that he makes his points without moralizing and without making his characters priggish. Cam and Rusty, the two young apprentices at war with authority, are frequently exasperating; they never fail to think and feel as boys do. Mr Armstrong clearly likes boys as much as he understands them, but his is a love without illusions. He knows just how mulish, perverse and wrong-headed a boy can be; he knows, too, from what deep causes these faults can spring, and he is slow to judge.

Sea Change is a book which had to be written. The author wrote it out of his own experiences at sea and out of his belief in the beauty, dignity and holiness of work. There is no romance, no glamour in *Sea Change*. It reveals the beauty of foreign ports, but also their heat and squalor. It does not hide the fact that work can be dull, back-breaking, disheartening. It shows above all how the life of a ship is the total of the lives of her crew, and what rich satisfaction there can be in subordinating oneself to the needs of the ship with intelligence, initiative, and humility.

from Chapter VII

While Rusty went aft to work with the carpenter, Cam was sent forrard with Calamity to rouse out a coil of manilla and start making cargo slings.

It was an interesting job and as usual the old sailor went out of his way to teach the boy all he could. They were mostly little things he passed on, such as the rule that to avoid kinks a coil of rope should always be used from the centre and never from the outside. But they were just those things that make a seaman and Cam stored them all away in his mind.

Calamity could see the lad was worked up about something, but behind the old sailor's long mournful face and drooping moustache a whole lot of wisdom hid and he said nothing. Instead he did his best to make Cam forget what was troubling him by talking about the sea and the islands that lay ahead.

The day had dawned clear and promised to be hot. The sky was a lighter blue than it had been, and as the sun rose higher it seemed to harden to a jade green at the horizon and filled with small white clouds moving slowly against the wind like an immense flock of sheep grazing on a hillside. The swell which had almost died away south of the Azores was picking up again and the ship pitched over it in long, lazy lurches. The sea was dark, shadowed by the rippling of the gentle south-east wind, but there was no gleam of a white-cap in all its wide expanse.

By breakfast time, thanks mainly to Calamity, Cam had himself under control again, . . .   *Sea Change*, p. 75

RICHARD ARMSTRONG comes from Tyneside. He worked as a boy in the steel works (the scene of his first novels) and went to sea after the First World War. After seventeen years he left the sea with a strong conviction of the need to write honestly and without sentimentality for boys. He has written successful adult novels. He lives now in the West Country.

SEA CHANGE

by RICHARD ARMSTRONG

Sea Change was the third of my books for boys and, in the writing of it, the broad idea that lies at the back of all my work in this field and gives it purpose and direction, came clear and was consciously applied for the first time.

That idea springs out of my own boyhood and in particular from the period of it when I stood on the edge of adolescence and began to be aware of life as a personal responsibility. In those days, like any child that ever was, I lived between two worlds – one, the real world with which I had to come to grips, and the other a dream world, the world I wanted to be, into which I retreated with all those things that were incomprehensible and made them tolerable by turning them into fantasy.

The real world was hard, uncompromising and bewildering. I needed desperately to understand it, to know the ways of it and what made it work. But while any number of grown-ups were willing to tell me *how* to do things, nobody ever took the trouble to explain *why* they should be done or to relate them to the life with which I had to come to terms. In consequence I learned *why* the hard way; down the years I groped for things I might otherwise have grasped with confidence; and I will never know just how much I have missed.

This was my starting point for *Sea Change*. It would have been so easy to pick up my reader in his dream world, to draw him a picture of life something like he imagined it there, but to do so would have been to lead him deeper into fantasy, to make reality so much more remote. My aim was the opposite. I wanted as far as possible to forearm the boy at the beginning of adolescence – not ramming a weapon into his hand willy-nilly, but showing him the size and shape of it and where it lies in such a way that he would take it up without realizing he was doing so and find himself using it when he needed to.

So in the book, I try to give him a factual picture of life as it comes at a boy in the Merchant Service, to make him familiar with the tools and instruments used there and show him how they fit into the general scheme of things. I bring him into contact with the kind of people he would meet and outline some of the problems and emotional conflicts he would have to face, the difficulties and the possibilities such a life would hold for him. And finally, I try, whether this is ultimately the line of activity he chooses to follow or not, to make him aware through it of his own power, his value as a human being; to give him confidence in himself, in the richness of life in the real world and his capacity for living it.

1949

AGNES ALLEN

The Story of Your Home

illustrations by Agnes and Jack Allen   FABER AND FABER

IN 1949, a year which produced several good novels, the Medal went to
an informative book. The reason was not hard to seek. *The Story of Your
Home* represented so precisely what librarians were looking for in the
imaginative treatment of a factual subject. Children are always ready to
learn about the world around them if they have an intelligent guide who
is neither condescending nor aggressively didactic. Mrs Allen was clearly
such a guide.

The *Story of Your Home* is a study in social, rather than architectural,
history. It is a history of homes, and not houses. Mrs Allen is much concerned with people; for her, changes in design or site must be considered
in terms of human comfort and convenience. She therefore takes a broad
view of her subject, and brings in a consideration of costume, tools,
furniture and decorations as well as the more permanent features of the
home. There is, consequently, a very real danger of crowding the story
with detail and confusing the reader with a multiplicity of facts; Mrs
Allen, however, is skilled in the selection of relevant detail. She keeps her
narrative alive with typical examples, but never allows the picture to
become muddled. This is a perspective of history.

Mrs Allen was fortunate in the collaboration of her husband in the
illustrations, and together they selected and simplified examples of buildings and their contents to bring out points in the text. The illustrations in
fact do 'illustrate'; they often make it possible to eliminate lengthy and
possibly confusing and tedious descriptions. The book is a good example
of the presentation of information to children. It has dignity and style,
and offers factual material simply but without condescension. It has
served as a model for many successful later series.

from Chapter XII

The big new houses of the eighteenth century generally had a private park or big garden round them, and these were as carefully designed as the houses themselves. The people who lived in the houses liked to have really fine views from their windows, so the landscape was often rearranged so that the view could be improved. Artificial lakes were made as well as lawns and drives, and trees were arranged in groups or in avenues, and statues and little buildings like Greek temples were put here and there.

Beautiful wrought-iron gates and railings were often set up. People no longer liked their own view to be cut off by a high wall, or their fine house to be hidden from other people so a new kind of wall, called a ha-ha, was invented. It was a wall or fence put at the bottom of a deep ditch, so that it was not visible from the house, but still prevented people from getting in.

One of the most famous of the new garden designers (or landscape gardeners, as they are called) was Lancelot Brown. He was generally called 'Capability' Brown, because when he was shown the landscape he was to work on he would nearly always say that he saw capabilities in it – meaning he thought he could make something of it.   *The Story of Your Home*, pp. 140–1

AGNES ALLEN has collaborated with her husband in a number of books introducing children in a persuasive and informal way to aspects of social, political and art history. She lives in Surrey.

THE STORY OF YOUR HOME

by AGNES ALLEN

I first thought of writing *The Story of Your Home* during the war. In the summer of 1943 or 1944 I spent a fortnight with my husband and son in a cottage in Oxfordshire which had been lent to us by relatives. Not far from the cottage were two curious little triangular erections which formed the entrance lodges to an estate. They naturally aroused the curiosity of my son, then aged about eleven. I told him that although these particular buildings were probably 'follies' built by some well-to-do man some time within the last two hundred years, centuries ago cottages in this form were quite common. I explained that countrymen made them by leaning two pairs of tree trunks towards each other a little distance apart, resting a ridge pole between them, and filling in the sides and ends with wattle and daub and anything else that came handy.

He seemed interested and surprised – and it suddenly occurred to me that thousands of children, like himself, were growing up in brick-built houses in which one turned a tap if one needed water, pressed a switch to flood a room with light, struck a match if one wanted to light a fire. Such things were, to them, so much a matter of course that they must find it very difficult to imagine what ordinary daily life was like in the past in homes that were so very different.

I decided then and there that I would write a book for children in which I would describe the ordinary homes of ordinary people at different periods, right back to the days when almost everything that made up the home, including the very house itself, was there only as a result of the personal exertions of the men and women who made up the household.

The middle of the war was not a good time to embark on the writing of a full-length book, so my first attempt was quite short – just a booklet of about twelve thousand words. While a publisher was brooding over this for nearly a year before returning it with polite regrets, I launched out on the writing and illustrating of a longer book dealing with the development of a typical English village, the idea for which had come to me while I was hunting out material for the booklet. It was only after this, *The Story of the Village*, and a further book, *The Story of Painting*, had been written and accepted for publication after the war ended, that I returned to the little book about homes.

I enlarged it to the dimensions of the other two full-length books – then re-wrote it all again because I did not like the first version – illustrated it with the help of my husband, and it was finally published in 1949, some five or six years after the idea for writing it first came to me.

1950

ELFRIDA VIPONT

The Lark on the Wing

illustrated by T. R. Freeman   OXFORD UNIVERSITY PRESS

ONE of the most individual books of 1948 was *The Lark in the Morn,*
which proved that in a master's hands even the school-story was not
extinct. It was a fresh, gay story, unerring in observation of school-girl
behaviour, and infused with a religious feeling which was as profound as
it was natural. At the end of the book Kit Haverard had finished her
school career realizing fully for the first time what part music must play
in her life. The book cried out for a sequel. When this came, in 1950, it
proved to be that rarest of all books, a sequel which grew naturally out of
the parent book and was completely true to it in spirit and in detail.

In *The Lark on the Wing* Kit has left school. Her plans for a career in
music are opposed by Laura, her competent and insensitive guardian (the
one outstandingly unsuccessful piece of characterization in this and the
earlier book). Kit has her way by an ingenious compromise, and the story
traces most beautifully her development as a singer and as a person. At
the end of the story she stands at the threshold of womanhood, quietly
confident, for she has laid the foundation of a good life.

'Goodness grows', says the frumpish and wise headmistress in *The Lark
in the Morn,* and that might be the motto of both books. Miss Vipont
never disguises her belief in goodness. Her books are not didactic, still less
priggish, but like a good Quaker she is aware of the 'Light Within' and
without affectation she makes spiritual growth the basis of her story. It
matters very much to her, and to her readers, that Kit should find herself
and remain true to herself, and in so doing not only become a great singer
but also fulfil the God within her.

This is a very serious and deeply moving book. It is also gay and
charming, and there is no contradiction in making Kit at once a serious
and a natural and ordinary girl. She is as much herself in spring-cleaning

the London flat as in penetrating with Papa Andreas the mysteries of *The Hill of the Lord*. She is a real person, a 'dratted little Quaker', and she is surrounded by friends of a lively individuality. The book gives a delightful picture of friendship in adolescence, drawn sympathetically but without sentimentality.

The Carnegie Medal was a tribute to Elfrida Vipont's fine understanding and her eloquent writing. It was a tribute, too, to the publishers, who designed the book with loving care and with due regard for its quality.

from Chapter VI

. . . Sir Hugh Cathcart had entered the room. The grand old composer was still an impressive sight, even in his extreme old age. Hair and beard were snowy white, and the once powerful shoulders were bowed. Increasing blindness did not detract from the nobility of his face; it had only increased that 'listening look' which had been noticeable even in his earlier days. He came forward now, a little uncertainly. 'Who is it, boy?' he asked.

'It's Kit Haverard, sir. You remember her, don't you? She's Tom's sister.'

'And Janey Kitson's daughter,' said Sir Hugh. 'I remember. You once sang in the Angel Trio and sent Papa Andreas and Terry out of their wits.'

He took Kit's place at the piano and began to play the Angel Trio softly. Kit sang the soprano part. It seemed the right thing to do. He made no comment as the loveliness died away. His fingers wandered over the keyboard till they found new music there. For a while he played something quite unfamiliar, hauntingly beautiful, and Kit felt a strange longing to share it with him as she had shared in the Angel Trio. Suddenly he broke off and his dim old eyes sought her face. 'That is your song,' he said.

The Lark on the Wing, p. 97

ELFRIDA VIPONT (Mrs Foulds) is a graduate of Manchester University; she studied singing in London and Paris, and became a professional singer. She is prominent in the Society of Friends and a tireless worker for many good causes. She writes also under the pseudonym of Charles Vipont. Her home is in Lancashire.

THE LARK ON THE WING

by ELFRIDA VIPONT

I have been asked to describe the events and ideas which led up to the writing of *The Lark on the Wing*. It should be an easy task and yet it is impossible. For *The Lark on the Wing* came into being because the characters in *The Lark in the Morn* went on living, and one cannot explain life. One can only enter into it, experience it and identify oneself with it, and that is what the author must do with the life of his creation. Life that is explicable pertains to this world only; such life belongs to 'the things which are seen', and like them it is temporal and fleeting. Creation in this medium is shallow and painless; it is only when the author, in so far as in him lies, occupies himself with 'the things which are not seen' that his work becomes on the one hand painful, because it is a giving of himself; and on the other hand deeply satisfying, because it is, even in a small measure and with all its imperfections, a reflection of eternal values.

Naturally, personal experiences enter in. 'Rosayac' is no one place in the Dordogne Valley, but it crystallizes a host of memories; I could pinpoint the moment when, all unconscious of the book which was to be written, I looked up at an old ruined castle guarding its tragic past and Rosayac was born. Lotte's Song is no one song that I have ever come across or sung; it is a distillation of all the love and all the loneliness and all the heartache in many folk songs I have known. Kit's experiences are not my experiences; the book would be a thin travesty of a photograph if they were. Fiction is not autobiography. Nevertheless, to re-read the book now recalls for me a host of memories – the essence is there, but not the substance. We distil in the crucible from our own experience a life which inspires the world of our creating. But the life of that world is not ours to shape; when our characters cease to be puppets they no longer dance to our bidding. And because we love our characters, we long to direct their steps in safety; I have tortured myself in vain to spare Kit or one of my other characters from the humiliation of failure. It is not easy for the author to realize that characters, like people, often learn from their mistakes.

Many of the characters in *The Lark on the Wing* were already in my mind before I wrote the book. I seldom lose the life of any of my characters; they simply go on growing. Some sprang into life as the book shaped itself in the early stages – Achille Pécaud came with Rosayac; Evelyn Hampson and Iris, Tante Anna and Lotte with Kit's London background; Bob Hardcastle after his brother Felix – I suppose it was typical of Bob's self-effacing character that he should dawn upon my mind long after his younger brother had pushed himself forward. Laurence Cray I cannot explain; if I could, he would be less real to me and his relationship with Milly less poignant. Chihar stands for all the far places where in loneliness of spirit men have dedicated their lives to 'the things which are unseen'.

The world of the two 'Lark' books goes on living in my mind with things past and things to come. I cannot distinguish between the life I have given it and the life it has given me. The memories it evokes still have their fragrance, like the rose petals in Janey's pot-pourri bowl, but keener than memory, and purer and more invigorating than its fragrance are the breezes which blow from the Hill of the Lord, where Laurence 'was part of a great multitude who had fought the good fight, fearing no evil, because they walked with God'.

1951

CYNTHIA HARNETT

The Wool-pack

illustrated by the author   METHUEN

HISTORICAL novels have been among the most successful children's books of the last twenty years. The best of these, even if they necessarily give story precedence over history, are not cloak-and-dagger or 'fancy-dress' romances but stories of everyday life in other times.

The change from Henty to Harnett is a significant one. It marks not only progress in historical writing but also a revolution in the teaching of history. The emphasis has moved from military and constitutional to social and economic, and modern children are expected to be familiar not with the tactics of Barnet or Marston Moor, but with the home life of the Elizabethans and the organization of the wool-trade. Miss Harnett's meticulous historical writing is the exact complement of class-room teaching; the fresh fluency of her style is, however, of the open-air as much as of the study, and children have not been misled into thinking of *The Wool-pack* as a 'school book'.

The Wool-pack is the story of Nicholas Fetterlock, son of a Cotswold wool-merchant of Burford at the end of the fifteenth century. He is a pleasant, ordinary boy with a lively interest in work and sport, and his intelligence helps him to protect his father from being ruined by Lombard money-lenders. A charming by-plot tells how he becomes reluctantly betrothed to Cecily, the daughter of a clothier of Newbury, and finds to his surprise that he becomes very fond of her.

This is a lively and eventful story, with plenty of action and excitement. It is also essentially a simple story, for the real theme, behind the manœuvres of Messer Antonio Bari, is that of the home-life of a successful merchant in England's principal industry. National prosperity was built on wool, and it is enormously interesting to see this prosperity at its source among the sheep-shearers on Cotswold and to follow it through

Southern England as Nicholas and his father ride through the narrow lanes from Burford to Southampton.

Miss Harnett, for all the fluency of her style, is a careful writer, and behind her book lies close and accurate research. She invents, but always on a basis of fact, and the richness of her understanding of Renaissance England is revealed not only in her descriptions but also in the many illustrations which illuminate the text. This is scholarship, lightly borne but nevertheless profound. The child who reads *The Wool-pack* as a delightful tale of adventure gains, incidentally, an insight into the age in which Modern England was born.

from Chapter VIII

The road, in places, was scarcely more than a grassy track, with hardened ruts suggesting that in winter it must be deep in mud. It sloped gently downhill as they left the Cotswolds behind them, and descended into the leafy depths of the Thames valley.

Here, through meadows deep in buttercups and ox-eyed daisies, they had to ride single file.

'One would never think,' Thomas Fetterlock remarked over his shoulder, 'that this is quite an important road. It leads to Radcot Bridge, where barges are loaded for Oxford and for London. It's a bad stretch in the winter – sticky clay, and ample cover for robbers.'

Glancing round him at the tangle of willows growing everywhere, Nicholas could well believe it. He wore, for the first time in his life, an anelace slung from his belt, and, even on this sunny morning he was glad to think of its broad sharp blade.

They plodded on at a walking pace, while the sun rose high in the heavens. Once they turned aside to hear Mass at a tiny village church, whose walls inside were completely covered with paintings, and the roof and arches with silver stars on a blue background, all very bright and gay. There seemed to be only a few cottages in the village, which was no more than a clearing in the wilderness.

The Wool-pack, p. 68

CYNTHIA HARNETT was trained as an artist, studying first at the Chelsea School of Art and then under her cousin, the late Vernon Stokes, with whom she collaborated in several picture books of country life. She lives in Berkshire, not far from the scene of *The Great House* and within reach of the Midland country in which her other books are set.

THE WOOL-PACK

by CYNTHIA HARNETT

IT is always difficult to trace the actual beginnings of an idea, particularly if it has laid dormant for half a lifetime. For the first idea of *The Wool-pack* I suppose I must go right back to my childhood, when I trailed happily at the heels of an elder brother who made a hobby of the sidelines of history. He took me out exploring old churches, rubbing brasses and hunting down heraldry. With him I learned to keep an ever-watchful eye for anything out of the way which might provide a clue in unfolding a story of the past; and which, incidentally, might earn me a pat on the back and an intoxicating 'good girl!' for my pains.

Among such finds were the brasses of the Cotswold wool merchants. They were ordinary enough people in their plain cloth gowns, but their calling was easy to spot because their feet rested either upon a sheep's back or on a sack of wool (a *sarpler* I should call it now!); and they used instead of a coat of arms, a cryptic merchants' mark. They rested as a rule in beautiful churches which they themselves had built out of the profits of the wool trade.

For many years these happy memories lay tucked away remotely in the back of my mind. I cherished all the while an ambition to write historical stories – writing stories and illustrating them had been another hobby encouraged in those early days – and I enjoyed writing for children. But somehow an initial impulse was lacking. The cloak and sword thriller held no attractions for me and I was tired to death of the boy who sailed with Drake or bowed his way as a page through the intricacies of dastardly plots against the Crown.

Then one day somebody said, 'It's odd that one never reads historical stories about *ordinary* people – ' (that, of course, was some years ago; one reads plenty of them now) – 'people who lived quiet normal lives and earned their living in ordinary ways.' That did it! The penny dropped! And yet even then the words Wool Trade did not instantly appear on the screen. I busied myself first with an architect's family in *The Great House*. It took Eileen Power's *Mediaeval People* to send me back hot foot to the Cotswolds. It was she who reminded me of the merchants of the wool staple with their fine stone houses and their lovely churches; she, too, who slipped in the thought of the possibility of a charming relationship between a boy and a girl betrothed in their childhood. And, into the bargain, all the weightier information contained in her books caused the machinery of the wool trade to turn over again so smoothly that Master Midwinter and his fellows seemed almost to rise from their brasses, pick up their sarplers and, twisting their signet rings on their fingers, imprint the canvas with their merchants' marks.

1952

MARY NORTON

The Borrowers

with illustrations by Diana Stanley   J. M. DENT

EVERY day people lose pins and needles, buttons, cotton reels, pen-nibs, and a great many other small things. Where does it all go, this vast assortment of oddments? In 1952 Mary Norton provided the answer. These things are borrowed.

In *The Borrowers* the Library Association honoured an entirely individual book. Mrs Norton owed something (as every writer of fantasy must) to E. Nesbit, but her treatment of a remarkable theme was highly personal. It is perhaps incorrect to describe the book as a fantasy. Once it is accepted that little people a few inches high may exist beneath the floor and behind the skirting-board, everything else in the story follows logically. Indeed, the remorseless logic which decreed that the Borrowers' lovely home must be destroyed has distressed some readers; it is however just and inevitable. There is a sadness in the story which comes from the view of a small civilization in decay, but the tragedy is kept in perspective through the author's device in telling her story second-hand, like an old half-forgotten tale.

Pod, Homily and little Arrietty (even their names are borrowed) live behind the clock, the last anxious survivors of a considerable colony of borrowers who had once lived in style. They exist in dread of cats and of being 'seen'. Arriety enlists the sympathies of a small boy staying in the house, and he brings them the contents of a doll's house until they enjoy unimagined luxury. Their hiding place is finally discovered by the housekeeper. What happens to the Borrowers when their home is destroyed is left uncertain (but Mrs Norton has set her readers' minds at rest in a sequel).

A simple story, but one worked out in exquisite detail and filled with wisdom and understanding. The writing has the precision and unemphatic

accuracy of miniature-painting, and this quiet certainty is mirrored in Miss Diana Stanley's illustrations which successfully translate into visual form the author's invention.

It would have been easy to make *The Borrowers* into a funny story. Mrs Norton has proved in other books that she has a genuine gift for comedy. She chose, however, to take her idea seriously, and in doing so she interpreted rightly the reactions of her audience. Children have been quick to recognize the authentic tone of this story, in which the author casts no covert glances at an adult listener, but speaks quietly and soberly, on equal terms with her readers.

from Chapter V

'What's the good,' asked Pod, 'of things behind glass?'

'Couldn't you break it?' suggested Arrietty. 'Just a corner, just a little tap, just a . . .' Her voice faltered as she saw the shocked amazement on her father's face.

'Listen here, Arrietty,' began Homily angrily, and then she controlled herself and patted Arrietty's clasped hands. 'She don't know much about borrowing,' she explained to Pod. 'You can't blame her.' She turned again to Arrietty. 'Borrowing's a skilled job, an art like. Of all the families who've been in this house, there's only us left, and do you know for why? Because your father, Arrietty, is the best borrower that's been known in these parts since – well, before your grandad's time. Even your Aunt Lupy admitted that much. When he was younger I've seen your father walk the length of a laid dinner-table, after the gong was rung, taking a nut or sweet from every dish, and down by a fold in the table-cloth as the first people came in at the door. He'd do it just for fun, wouldn't you, Pod?'

Pod smiled wanly. 'There weren't no sense in it,' he said.

'Maybe,' said Homily, 'but you did it! Who else would dare?'

'I were younger then,' said Pod. He sighed and turned to Arrietty. 'You don't break things, lass. That's not the way to do it. That's not borrowing . . .' *The Borrowers*, pp. 37–8

MARY NORTON started as an actress at the Old Vic, but left the stage on marriage, when she went to live in Portugal. She has four children. She had a great and lasting success in 1945 with her first book for children *The Magic Bedknob*, which introduced an immortal character in Miss Price, the learner-witch. The story was continued in *Bonfire and Broomsticks*. Mrs Norton has lived in Chelsea for a number of years.

ABOUT BORROWERS
by MARY NORTON

I think the first idea – or first feeling – of the Borrowers came through my being short-sighted: when others saw the far hills, the distant woods, the soaring pheasant, I, as a child, would turn sideways to the close bank, the tree roots and the tangled grasses. Moss, fern-stalks, sorrel stems, created the *mise en scène* for a jungle drama, lacking in those days its dramatis personae. But one invented the characters – small, fearful people picking their way through miniature undergrowth; one saw smooth places where they might sit and rest: branched stems which might invite them to climb: sandy holes into which they might creep for shelter.

All childhood has its lonely periods – the brisk 'run-out-and-play' of harassed grown-ups: the 'stay-there-till-we-come-for-you' of elder brothers: and it was later I invented, for the sake of companionship, a way to people this tiny Eden. In those days before the First World War, one could buy small, china dolls with movable arms and flaxen hair, naked except for shoes and socks which were painted on. They stood about three or four inches high and were on sale among the lollipops in every village shop. It took no time at all to dress and disguise these and to assign to each its role. Water-colour, silver paint, odd pieces of coloured silk, tufts of black fur from a hearth rug – and here were one's puppets made. Infinitely docile, they played out great dramas for a child's entertainment, on smooth stages of sun-dried rock or among the green-lit shadows of the bracken . . . knights, ladies, fairies, witches. Joan of Arc was burned once, I remember, tied to her stake amid faggots of pine-needles. What a fire was there – with tears from me – while the bishops stood around.

On the days when one was confined to the house, imagined excursions took place among the chair-legs and across the deep pile of the carpets. Here, the hazards were even greater: hearth and fire-irons for these tiny people took on almost nightmare properties. The sideboard, too, with its gleaming slippery silver, was rather frightening. No wonder they took to mouse-holes and the wainscot, creating their own small safety.

Children nowadays are encouraged to invent, but still in ways devised by adults. 'Clear-up-that-mess' has destroyed many a secret world. As the Borrowers' house was destroyed by Mrs Driver. This particular incident, oddly enough, worries grown-ups far more than it does children. Children are used to repeated small destructions – in the name of punctuality or tidiness – and have learned to accept them. If the raw materials are there to hand, they simply build again. Grown-ups, faced with equivalent disaster, make far more fuss. Sometimes, perhaps, we should think about this . . .

1953

EDWARD OSMOND

A Valley Grows Up

illustrated by the author   OXFORD UNIVERSITY PRESS

ONE of the most difficult, and fundamental, problems in the teaching of history is that of how to give to children a sense of the panorama of Time. Children are quick to enjoy the drama of the past and to acquire a visual appreciation of its colour, they delight in unfamiliar costumes and fashions and in the strange shapes of buildings and landscapes. They learn history, however, as a series of unrelated episodes, and find it hard to see history in perspective as a sequence of change, development and regression.

Many teachers and writers have appreciated and tried to solve this problem, few more successfully than Mr Edward Osmond in *A Valley Grows Up*. Mr Osmond enjoyed one advantage, possibly two. He was an artist, and could invent, in line, visual symbols which made a more immediate impact than could the most accurate verbal description. He was, moreover, not a professional historian, and could approach his subject without prejudice or preconceptions. He also had a quite remarkable gift for clear precise prose.

A Valley Grows Up is the story of an imaginary landscape through seventy centuries. The text is based on ten oil-paintings, printed as double-spreads, each of which captures a moment of history at one of the great turning points from the Stone Age to the height of Victorian prosperity. The paintings show the rise and fall of civilizations, the change in fashions and styles of buildings and in the habits and occupations of the inhabitants of Dungate, the little town which grows so naturally and so beautifully at the crossing of the river. In a series of line drawings the author brings the reader closer to the town to show some of the individual buildings and people. The accompanying text modestly draws attention to the details of the drawings and to the social and political and economic factors which have brought about the changes. Mr Osmond is an excellent and unobtrusive guide. He never says too much or labours a point, but in word, as well as line, he keeps the same admirable sense of proportion.

It was unfortunate, if inevitable, that in reproduction the original pictures lost much of their definition and their detail. The reader sometimes looks in vain for a feature mentioned in the text but reduced into invisibility by the block-maker.

In awarding the Medal to Mr Osmond for *A Valley Grows Up*, the Library Association recognized a notable essay in the imaginative interpretation of history, a book which is immediately attractive and continuously absorbing, and which brilliantly and successfully simplifies a complex subject. In an age which goes in much for 'digested' knowledge, it is agreeable to have so admirable and authentic an example.

Extract

In the town there are numerous fine houses and several large inns. You will notice many tall chimneys now, a sure sign of increased comfort. Windows too are larger, as glass is more plentiful, the newer houses showing many projecting oriel windows which have become very popular. Thatch is still used a lot as a roofing material; but the oak shingles of past years are becoming rare, for the woodlands are now much reduced, since so much land was cleared for sheep-raising, and timber has been lavishly used for fuel. These shingles have been replaced by tiles; while on the stone-built houses stone slates are sometimes used, and lead is still found on the most important buildings.

Turning now from the houses of the ordinary people, I must mention the most remarkable change of all: the monks have gone. This happened about sixty years ago when Henry VIII closed down all the abbeys; and already the two abbeys in the valley are in ruins, and the little friary has disappeared. At Bemmer Minster the new manor house is built of stones taken from the Abbey buildings; and lead from their roofs and other useful materials have been carted off and sold by the man who now owns the place. The remainder of the buildings have been left to decay, which is not a slow process now that the protecting roofs have been removed. The chancel of the great church has been preserved as a village church, and the great barn and other useful buildings are being kept in repair and are now farm buildings and cottages; but grass and weeds have soon grown where the monks once worshipped, and young trees have taken root in the walls and are prizing open the joints of the masonry so carefully built by the skilled masons of medieval times. Beautifully carved bosses and finials from the church and cloisters lie about among the weeds, and birds build their nests up against the fast fading pictures of saints and prophets.

A Valley Grows Up, pp. 61–4

EDWARD OSMOND was born in Suffolk in 1900. His work as a teacher of illustration in London gave him the original idea for *A Valley Grows Up*. He has also written books for the Batsford 'Junior Heritage' series, and, in collaboration with Mrs Osmond, a history of the Thames.

A VALLEY GROWS UP
by EDWARD OSMOND

Everyone has probably wished, when visiting some historic place, that they could go back in time and see it again as it was in years gone by. I can remember wishing ardently to be able to do just that on many occasions in my own childhood. When standing among the grass-grown mounds which marked the site of a lonely abbey, perhaps, or a deserted village, I would try to re-create the place in my imagination as it had once been. But at best I could only see it as it was in its last heyday. I wanted to go over the whole process of its growth, from the time when there was nothing to be seen there but the native briars and bracken.

Later I developed another wish – to be able to conjure up a continuous mental picture of all the longer phases of history – to be able to run off, in my mind, a kind of film, giving a broad, four-dimensional record of the great movements and tendencies in past times. I think I first became conscious of my own need of this when, as a student, I began a course in art history, and found that I possessed no continuous mental back-cloth against which to view all the personalities and schools of painting that I then met.

After World War II, I was called on to help students who, through war-time deficiencies in their schooling, were in far worse plight than my own. Realizing their difficulties, I illustrated my lectures by means of an imaginary village which, together, we created 'from scratch'. I was surprised at the strong impression that this left in the minds of the students; and I was even more surprised at the great affection that we all seemed to develop for this place, although it had its only existence in a series of week-by-week blackboard drawings.

72

However, for many years before that I had been working on and off with a view to developing something of this kind for use in schools. And eventually I put my thoughts down as rough drawings for what I felt might be a useful series of school wall-charts, hoping that some teacher of history might be commissioned to write a short handbook to accompany them. I then went in search of a publisher.

I showed my roughs first to Mr Bell, who was then children's editor at the Oxford University Press – fortunately they never had to travel any further.

At a second meeting I learnt that wall charts were out of the question, owing to the curious working of purchase tax; but Mr Bell was eager to proceed with my idea in book form, and insisted that I should write the book.

The new idea filled me with misgivings. However, my children's editor, for all his gentleness, was a very determined man. So, after many months, the work was complete; but the usual process was reversed – illustrations first, text following them and, at the very last moment, the title of the book.

1954

RONALD WELCH

Knight Crusader

illustrated by William Stobbs   OXFORD UNIVERSITY PRESS

THE FIRST historical novel to receive the Carnegie Medal was a story of
home-life in a setting which, though strange, was linked by many ideas,
beliefs and manners with the modern world. The second showed an age
which was remote and almost entirely alien. Both novels described
Christian communities it is true, but there is little similarity between the
Christianity of the Crusaders and that of either the Cotswold woolmen
or Miss Vipont's twentieth-century Quakers.

Knight Crusader is a story of the Frankish Kingdom of Outremer which
had been founded after the success of the First Crusade. By the last quarter
of the twelfth century the realm is beginning to break up through internal
dissention as much as through the attacks of Saladin's Turks. The hero of
Mr Welch's story is a young knight, of Norman descent but born in
Outremer, who becomes involved in the disastrous march on Damascus
which culminated in the destruction of the Crusaders' army at the battle
of Hattin. Like all Mr Welch's heroes, Philip is a tough warrior, but his
courage and ferocity are matched with intelligence; and he makes his way
through enemy territory to join ultimately in the Third Crusade. This
enables the writer to give an attractive, and convincing, portrait of
Richard Cœur-de-Lion. In a final section of the book, the hero returns,
a battle-scarred veteran, to claim his inheritance in Wales.

Mr Welch's is a novel of action. It contains two major battles, many
skirmishes, a single-combat, an attempted assassination, a joust, and lastly
the successful assault of a castle. All of these are described with great vigour
and understanding of the technique of conflict. They also come naturally
from the conditions of the age. The author is familiar with the atmosphere
of twelfth-century Jerusalem, with its curious mixture of elegance and
brutality, and he points the contrast between the civilized manners of the

Eastern knights and the rough ill-breeding of most of the Europeans. He shows the sowing of some of the seeds from which the culture of the later Middle Ages was to spring.

Physically, *Knight Crusader* was most distinguished, with noble drawings by William Stobbs and an appropriately dignified format. Not for the first time, the Carnegie Medal paid tribute not only to the author but also to the publisher who had given the story so handsome a dress.

from Chapter XV

He was surrounded once more by the dark, snarling faces, white turbans and steel helmets, the gaping, red nostrils of frightened horses. In a frenzy of hatred and fury he cut, stabbed, and hacked until he had cleared a space, as Richard was doing on his left.

Into those two narrow gaps the leading English and Norman knights hurled their weight and speed, and behind the two raging figures that led them, they split the Mamelukes into small, struggling groups, cut their way through, then turned and annihilated Saladin's picked men.

Philip suddenly realized that it was all over. Through his eye-slits he saw a distant mob of panic-stricken horsemen racing for the shelter of the forest. He drooped wearily in his saddle, his body glowing with heat, his face dripping with perspiration. His breath came in harsh sobs of exhaustion as he felt the weight of his shoulder straps dragged down by the shield. Even the sword seemed a dead weight in his hand, and his fingers on the hilt were trembling with fatigue.

Slowly he sheathed the long blade and tugged at his helm. He could see the blue sea, and the ships beating in towards the beach. The plain was littered with the debris of the battle, the piles of horses and men, the spent arrows, the swords dropped in flight, the shields and dust-covered evidence of what had happened in those last furious minutes.

Knight Crusader, pp. 214–16

RONALD WELCH (R. O. Felton) comes from Wales, and his interest in the Principality is mirrored in all his books. He taught history at Berkhamsted and Bedford, and is now the headmaster of Okehampton Grammar School, Devon.

KNIGHT CRUSADER
by RONALD WELCH

The Crusades have always fascinated me, and particularly the great Norman castles which still stand, so strangely out of place, in the mountains of Judea and Syria. When I started to write books for children, a story with the Crusades as a background was one that appealed to me immediately, but I was deterred by the difficulty of describing a country I had never visited, and as I now live on the edge of Dartmoor, the lack of a good reference library near at hand was a further handicap. So I wrote a story about a Welsh castle with which I was familiar, and this was published by the Oxford University Press. Encouraged by this, I decided to have a go at the Crusader story.

I made a list of suitable books, and sent it without much hope to the County Library at Exeter. To my astonishment, for I was shamefully ignorant of what County Libraries can do, books descended upon me from all parts of England. I spent three happy months making notes, several hundred pages of them; I pored over large-scale maps of the Near East; I read travel books about Palestine, and histories of the Mahommedans, and I even delved into the Koran, though I must admit that I was not much the wiser for that.

My publishers made many suggestions about altering the book when they received it, and I re-wrote the entire story, typing it painfully with two fingers, until my interest in the Crusades waned considerably. However, this time the book was accepted and published, and I was fortunate in the artist, William Stobbs, who drew many forceful and delightful pictures, including a very striking dust cover.

When I was writing, I realized that the historical background would be unfamiliar to many children, so I tried it out at various stages on my daughter, adding more detail to make the picture clearer. The greatest difficulty, though, and one that must occur to all writers of historical fiction for children, is to decide how much of this background should be included. For instance, by our standards the medieval world was brutal, coarse and filthy. How much of this should I tell children? Again, as military history is my chief hobby, I wanted to include some battles, and though battles are exciting enough to read about, they are also bloody and horrifying in detail. So I tried to strike a reasonable balance, and the Oxford University Press made no comments; nor did any of the reviews at the time.

Quite recently a long article on the Carnegie Medal books appeared in a literary paper, and I was startled to see *Knight Crusader* described as 'sickeningly bloody', and the background of a complexity quite beyond the ordinary boy or girl.

As a teacher and writer of history I find this point of view both depressing and retrograde. I know from my own experience that children detest people who talk or write down to them; they are eager to accept the challenge of a more adult approach, and they can read quite enough stories about the more popular periods of history, though there are several other writers besides myself who have dealt with the lesser known episodes. Surely, children who read historical fiction do so because they are interested in history, besides wanting to read a story, and they are therefore anxious to learn. But this reviewer, instead of urging us to give children something into which they can put their teeth, is telling us to provide them with a succession of feeding bottles.

I do hold very strongly that it is wrong to try and fool children with the idea that the people of the past lived in a romantic and delightful world. They did not, and the truth is invariably more interesting than the legend. In any case, children who have no liking for history will never bother to read any of my books, so there is not much point in my writing stories for non-existent readers.

1955

ELEANOR FARJEON

The Little Bookroom: Eleanor Farjeon's short stories for children chosen by herself

illustrated by Edward Ardizzone OXFORD UNIVERSITY PRESS

BY a curious chance it was not until 1955 that an opportunity came to honour the writer who, after the death of Walter de la Mare, was the last survivor of the golden age of children's literature. No award of the Carnegie Medal gave more general delight and satisfaction than that to Eleanor Farjeon for a collection of short stories which so effectively summed up a lifetime of work for children.

GENEROUS as Miss Farjeon is to all who associate with her, she has always been particularly good to her illustrators, inspiring them to their finest work. Of all her books, *The Little Bookroom* shows most clearly the happy collaboration

78

of writer and artist. It has seemed appropriate, therefore, to ask Mr Ardizzone for some impressions of his work on this book, which so richly deserved its medal and the Hans Christian Andersen Medal which recognized its pre-eminence among the children's books of the world. The latter award was particularly fitting, for of all modern writers Eleanor Farjeon is closest to Andersen in poetry, fantasy, pathos and humour.

ON ILLUSTRATING MISS FARJEON'S WORK
by EDWARD ARDIZZONE

As a child before the 1914 War I lived with my family in a Suffolk village. Telephones and cars were few; the cinema was hardly known and the radio not at all. It was still the world of the horse, with the pony trap, governess cart and wagonette much in evidence.

It was also for us a small world bounded by the village and its surrounding fields, and one in which we made most of our own amusements. There were the plays which we wrote and in which we acted and the family magazine, highly illustrated by me, to which every member of the family, young and old, contributed. We read much and knew and loved the works of Hans Andersen, Grimm, Charlotte Yonge, Mrs Ewing, and other nursery classics. We played long and elaborate games of make believe, and then, too, there were the rural tasks such as helping with hay and harvest. We were very young and it is only fair to admit that our mother was behind much of our more ambitious activities.

You will see that though our world was small it was a busy one, but what I think was special about it, was that in the realms of the imagination it was a very wide and spacious world indeed.

Now the point I wish to make is that on reading Miss Farjeon's stories I was immediately transported back into this old imaginary world of ours. It was as if some responsive chord had been struck. To put it vulgarly, the stories clicked. They were stories that were somehow both new and fresh, yet to me familiar.

I also found something else in these stories which was important to me as an illustrator. It was the poetic quality.

Miss Farjeon is a poetess and her prose is a poet's prose. It is sparing in description. One might say that she hardly describes at all, and yet, owing to that magic which belongs to poetry, each sentence or paragraph is evocative of a very precise visual image. It is a prose which never leaves one in doubt as to its meaning.

I would like to quote a passage from *The Little Bookroom* to make my meaning clear, but alas, can find none short enough for the space at my disposal!

However, take the opening of the story called 'Young Kate'. Miss Daw lived in a narrow house on the edge of the town and young Kate was her little servant. Now it was a tall house because one is told it had an attic and it was a cliff-like house because houses on the edge of a town have a cliff-like quality. Besides it was inhabited by Miss Daw and Daws are cliff-dwelling birds. From the attic Kate could see all the meadows that lay outside the town, and that must have been a wide vista indeed.

But doesn't this conjure up an exact picture clear and sharp in the mind? I can hardly see how it can fail to do so.

Now what more can an illustrator ask of his author's work than this evocative quality plus an imagery in key with his own? Given this, stories almost illustrate themselves, invention is no labour, only drawing remains to be done and that is the least of our difficulties, and work becomes a joy. MISS FARJEON HAS IT ALL.

from *The Barrel-organ*

'But who's to dance?' asked the Traveller again.

'There's no want of dancers in a wood,' said the Organ-grinder, and turned his handle.

As soon as the tune started, the Traveller felt the grass and leaves flutter as before, and in a moment the air was full of moths and fireflies, and the sky was full of stars, come out to dance like children in a back street. And it seemed to the Traveller, by the light of the dancing stars, that flowers came up in the wood where a moment before there had been none, pushing their way in haste through the moss to sway to the tune on their stalks, and that two or three little streams began to run where a moment before they had been still. And the Traveller thought there were other things dancing that he couldn't see, as well as flowers and streams and stars and moths and flies and leaves in the night. The wood was quite full of dancing from top to toe, and it was no longer dark, for the moon had hopped out of a cloud, and was gliding all over the sky.

The Little Bookroom, pp. 118–19

ELEANOR FARJEON has written the story of her childhood in *A Nursery in the Nineties*. As a member of a most talented family she grew up in the artistic and literary life of England and America. Her brothers made distinctive contributions to music, literature and the theatre. Miss Farjeon has known almost every contemporary writer worth knowing. Among her greatest friends were Walter de la Mare and Edward Thomas. In poetry, plays and stories she is second only to De la Mare among modern writers for children. Her home is in Hampstead.

THE LITTLE BOOKROOM

by ELEANOR FARJEON

'There's no use trying,' said Alice to the Red Queen, 'one *can't* believe impossible things' – and when you ask how I came to write *The Little Bookroom* what can I say but 'One *can't* answer impossible questions, there's no use trying.'

However, the Red Queen, who no doubt could have answered Six Impossible Questions before breakfast, advised Alice to draw a long breath, and shut her eyes – so here goes.

The Little Bookroom is not a story, it is twenty-seven stories, and it is simple enough to explain how, having written them over a stretch of thirty years, I came to collect them from their various sources under a composite title, added several others, and wrote a little preface to account for their variety. Most of the seeds from which the twenty-seven grew are unknown to me; they blew from anywhere or nowhere into the fertilizing soil of the imagination which is beyond analysis. But here are some dozen I can put my finger on.

In 1945, when 'The Glass Slipper' was running at the St James's Theatre, I made friends with the little Irish commissionaire who fetched up the taxicabs; during our many chats between shows he spoke of his small son, the apple of his eye, for whom he vamped up incredible tales about the land the child had never seen. *The Connemara Donkey* was not one of the little man's tales, but it was born of those talks. One Twelfth Night when the holly in my house had been banished, I walked out with my tiny Christmas tree decorated with tinsel and 'brights' – in a poor alley near by a little girl gasped 'Ooh!'; I gave her the tree and presently wrote *The Glass Peacock*. When *I* was a little girl my favourite treat in Margate was to buy a penny fortune from a gypsy's love-bird, like Susan Brown in *The Lovebirds*, and when my niece Joan was a still littler girl, demanding stories to be made up on the spur of the moment, *The Lady's Room* became a smash-hit and had to be repeated for a run of quite two years. Later on I was able to write *that* one down without thinking. Curious paragraphs in the corners of newspapers lodged themselves in corners of my mind: the bringing home to England of corn from an Egyptian tomb: the tearful farewell kisses on their fruit-trees of Sicilian peasants fleeting from Etna's stream of lava: the mention of a Russian sentryman who turned out every day to walk so many paces to nowhere and back again, obeying an obsolete order long forgotten: out of these tiny suggestions came *The King and the Corn*, *The Girl who Kissed the Peach-Tree*, and *In Those Days*. A friend woke up one morning in my house from a dream of an unhappy miser who, attacked by a fit of charity, ended his life in happy poverty. This was *The Kind Farmer*. One day in Horsham Station I put my penny into the platform-ticket-machine while a small boy put his into the chocolate-slot-machine – how tragic, I thought, if he had posted his penny in *my* machine by mistake! There's *Pennyworth*. *The Clumber Pup?* I knew and loved a Clumber pup half-a-century ago, and long after he was dead he wanted to be put into a story. *Leaving Paradise?* One summer in Normandy I met Geneviève who didn't believe in fairies, and Yvonne who did. And *Pannychis?* No, never mind about that one, its seed is not to be fingered.

Well, there's a handful of them traced to their sources – my breath has run out, I've opened my eyes, and still I don't know How.

1956

C. S. LEWIS

The Last Battle: a story for children

illustrated by Pauline Baynes THE BODLEY HEAD

ONE of the literary events of 1950 was the publication of *The Lion, the Witch and the Wardrobe*, an allegorical fantasy by Dr C. S. Lewis which was at once stimulating, puzzling, highly exciting and, for some sensitive adult readers, distressing. It opened the door into the enchanted kingdom of Narnia. In each succeeding year Dr Lewis released a further communiqué from this distant country, and in 1956 he brought the story to a close in apocalyptic fashion with the story of the destruction of Narnia and the translation of the chosen people to a promised land, the Narnia of the spirit. In awarding the Carnegie Medal to Dr Lewis for *The Last Battle*, the Library Association no doubt had the whole series in mind, and wished to pay tribute to a creative effort of the imagination which was as powerful as it was consistent.

The Narnia stories are 'moral' tales, but in them morality and narrative are so closely related that it is impossible to separate them. They have grown together in the writer's mind. It is Dr Lewis's strength that he is both Christian apologist and skilled story-teller. The stories are full of action, described in lively detail, with drama and humour. If they look back to George Macdonald, there are few better models in fantastic writing; if they owe much to E. Nesbit, that is a debt shared by almost every writer for children in this century; they have, moreover, a quality all their own, deriving from Dr Lewis's richly stored mind and his deeply pondered beliefs. No books are, in the fullest sense, more personal.

Narnia is a kingdom in a world not our own, but one to which humans may, under certain conditions and when they are needed, go. At successive crises, when the forces of evil seem likely to prevail, some of the Sons of Adam and the Daughters of Eve bring their courage and their simplicity to the support of Aslan, the great lion who is God. In *The Last Battle* the war between good and evil is nearing its end. To the reader's surprise, evil seems to prevail, but in a remarkable and powerfully written epilogue the author shows how unimportant earthly victory and defeat can be. The Narnia which had been destroyed 'was only a shadow or a copy of the real Narnia which has always been here and always will be here'.

For children, the inner meaning of these stories may be only dimly understood, or understood imaginatively rather than intellectually; but few children can remain unmoved by the magnificent scenes of action, or the lively and odd characters, or the wonderful timing of suspense and climax, or the colourful and romantic settings. At a time when narrative is in general the weakest feature of contemporary fiction, Dr Lewis shows in the Narnia stories that he is a story-teller in the authentic tradition.

The Last Battle, like the other Narnia novels, is illustrated by Pauline Baynes, an illustrator whose delicate, flexible and imaginative style matches remarkably the varied tones of the author's fancy. These are definitive illustrations.

from Chapter VIII

He alighted on a rocky crag a few feet from Tirian, bowed his crested head, and said in his strange eagle's-voice, 'Hail, King'.

'Hail, Farsight,' said Tirian. 'And since you call me King, I may well believe you are not a follower of the Ape and his false Aslan. I am right glad of your coming.'

'Sire,' said the Eagle, 'when you have heard my news you will be sorrier of my coming than of the greatest woe that ever befell you.'

Tirian's heart seemed to stop beating at these words, but he set his teeth and said 'Tell on'.

'Two sights have I seen,' said Farsight. 'One was Cair Paravel filled with dead Narnians and living Calormenes: The Tisroc's banner advanced upon your royal battlements: and your subjects flying from the city – this way and that, into the woods. Cair Paravel was taken from the sea. Twenty great ships of Calormen put in there in the dark of the night before last night.'

No one could speak.

'And the other sight, five leagues nearer than Cair Paravel, was Roonwit the Centaur lying dead with a Calormene arrow in his side. I was with him in his last hour and he gave me this message to your Majesty: to remember that all worlds draw to an end and that noble death is a treasure which no one is too poor to buy.'

'So, ' said the King, after a long silence, 'Narnia is no more.'

The Last Battle, pp. 94–5

CLIVE STAPLES LEWIS was born in 1898. He served in the Somerset Light Infantry in the First World War, at the end of which he went as a Scholar to University College, Oxford. After an exceptionally brilliant career at the University he became a lecturer at his own College, and later became Fellow and Tutor of Magdalen College. He finally left Oxford to become Professor of Medieval and Renaissance English at Cambridge. His many writings reflect his interest in theology, scholarship and moral philosophy. *The Screwtape Letters* (1942), an ingenious study of the nature of good and evil, is perhaps the most successful of his books, although his trilogy of romantic fantasies for adults has had many admirers.

Dr Lewis gave an outstandingly wise and witty paper at the Bournemouth Conference of the Library Association in 1952. From this address he has adapted the following extract illustrating his attitude towards writing for children.

ONE WAY OF WRITING FOR CHILDREN

by C. S. LEWIS

In a certain sense, I have never exactly 'made' a story. With me the process is much more like bird-watching than like either talking or building. I see pictures. Some of these pictures have a common flavour, almost a common smell, which groups them together. Keep quiet and watch and they will begin joining themselves up. If you were very lucky (I have never been as lucky as all that) a whole set might join themselves so consistently that there you had a complete story: without doing anything yourself. But more often (in my experience always) there are gaps. Then at last you have to do some deliberate inventing, have to contrive reasons why these characters should be in these various places doing these various things. I have no idea whether this is the usual way of writing stories, still less whether it is the best. It is the only one I know: images always come first.

. . . The question 'What do modern children need?' will not lead you to a good moral. If we ask that question we are assuming too superior an attitude. It would be better to ask 'What moral do I need?' for I think we can be sure that what does not concern us deeply will not deeply interest our readers, whatever their age. But it is better not to ask the question at all. Let the pictures tell you their own moral. For the moral inherent in them will rise from whatever spiritual roots you have succeeded in striking during the whole course of your life. But if they don't show you any moral, don't put one in. For the moral you put in is likely to be a platitude, or even a falsehood, skimmed from the surface of your consciousness. It is impertinent to offer the children that. For we have been told on high authority that in the moral sphere they are probably at least as wise as we. Anyone who *can* write a children's story without a moral, had better do so: that is, if he is going to write children's stories at all. The only moral that is of any value is that which arises inevitably from the whole cast of the author's mind.

Indeed, everything in the story should arise from the whole cast of the author's mind. We must write for children out of those elements in our own imagination which we share with children: differing from our child readers not by any less, or less serious, interest in the things we handle, but by the fact that we have other interests which children would not share with us. The matter of our story should be a part of the habitual furniture of our minds. . . . Nothing seems to me more fatal, for this art, than an idea that whatever we share with children is, in the derogatory sense, 'childish', and that whatever is childish is somehow comic. We must meet children as equals in that area of our nature where we are their equals. Our superiority consists partly in commanding other areas, and partly (which is more relevant) in the fact that we are better at telling stories than they are. The child as reader is neither to be patronized nor idolized: we talk to him as man to man. But the worst attitude of all would be the professional attitude which regards children in the lump as a sort of raw material which we have to handle. We must of course try to do them no harm: we may, under the Omnipotence, sometimes dare to hope that we may do them good. But only such good as involves treating them with respect. We must not imagine that we are Providence or Destiny. I will not say that a good story for children could never be written by someone in the Ministry of Education, for all things are possible. But I should lay very long odds against it.

Once in a hotel dining room I said, rather too loudly, 'I loathe prunes'. 'So do I' came an unexpected six-year-old voice from another table. Sympathy was instantaneous. Neither of us thought it funny. We both knew that prunes are far too nasty to be funny. That is the proper meeting between man and child as independent personalities. Of the far higher and more difficult relations between child and parent or child and teacher, I say nothing. An author, as a mere author, is outside all that. He is not even an uncle. He is a freeman and an equal, like the postman, the butcher, and the dog next door.

from *On three ways of writing for children*, by C. S. Lewis. L.A. Proceedings of the Annual Conference, Bournemouth, 1952.

ANOTHER MEDAL

THE terms of reference for the Carnegie Medal Sub-committee lay emphasis on the importance of good format in the production of books for children, and the chosen books have all reached a very satisfactory standard of physical excellence. Even in the war years it was possible to choose books which showed dignity, style and good taste in layout, typography and illustration, although format was no doubt one of the considerations which weighed with the Sub-committee in withholding an award in 1943 and 1945.

Illustration has always been an important element in the design of books for children, and it is appropriate that the Medal-winning books, chosen as they were primarily for their literary qualities, yet represent the best in modern book-illustration. Nearly a third are illustrated by their authors, and the harmony between text and drawing in, for example, *The Woolpack*, shows clearly how valuable the possession of artistic skill can be to a writer. Other books have for their illustrators artists like Robert Gibbings and Edward Ardizzone who have won distinction in many different fields, as well as others, like C. Walter Hodges, who are best known for their work in children's books.

The importance of the illustrator, whose best work may well be in books which are not eligible for consideration for the Carnegie Medal, prompted the Library Association in 1955 to institute a new award, the Kate Greenaway Medal, to be given for an outstanding work of illustration. Of the great Victorian triumvirate of picture-book makers, Randolph Caldecott had already been pressed into service for an American Medal, and the passage of time had reduced the stature of Walter Crane; Kate Greenaway, whose books were always so admirable in design as well as pictorially delightful, was a highly satisfactory choice for the naming of a Medal of which she would so wholeheartedly have approved. The new medal, for which Mr Reginald H. Hill, M.S.I.A., N.R.D., made a very fine design, was withheld in its first year, and awarded for the first time to Mr Edward Ardizzone for *Tim All Alone* (Oxford University Press, 1956).

No award could have been more appropriate, for Mr Ardizzone had, since the publication of *Little Tim and the Brave Sea Captain* in 1936, been the criterion of excellence in the English picture-book, bringing to the medium a peculiarly English style and inspiration to resist the very strong influences from the United States and France. Mr Ardizzone is an artist in the great tradition deriving from Rowlandson. His highly individual style has been put at the service of Thackeray and Trollope, Villon and De la Mare, Eleanor Farjeon and James Reeves, but his most characteristic, and in many ways his most successful work, is in the series of picture-books, to his own text, which follow the fortunes of little Tim, that intrepid but modest seaman. With *Tim All Alone* Mr Ardizzone brought the series to a conclusion. It gave great satisfaction to his many admirers not only that he should receive recognition for his work but also that the Greenaway Medal should be awarded for a book which so delightfully exhibited his individual qualities at their best: *Tim All Alone* has by right a place beside *The Three Jovial Huntsmen*, *A-Apple Pie*, *Johnny Crow's Garden* and *Peter Rabbit* on the shelf reserved for picture-books which represent at its best the English tradition.